G R A P H I S   T Y P O G R A P H Y   2

75 YEARS OF BAUHAUS DESIGN 1919 1994

GRAPHIS TYPOGRAPHY 2

. . . .

AN INTERNATIONAL SELECTION OF THE BEST IN TYPOGRAPHIC DESIGN

PUBLISHER AND CREATIVE DIRECTOR: B. MARTIN PEDERSEN

EDITORS: CLARE HAYDEN, HEINKE JENSSEN

ASSOCIATE EDITOR: PEGGY CHAPMAN

PRODUCTION DIRECTORS/DESIGNERS: JOHN JEHEBER, JENNIFER RUF

GRAPHIS INC.

OPPOSITE • DESIGN BY KNOLL GRAPHICS

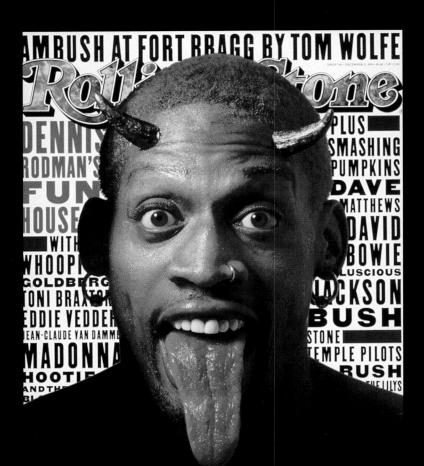

CONTENTS

ISBN 1-888001-26-7 © COPYRIGHT UNDER UNIVERSAL COPYRIGHT CONVENTION • COPYRIGHT © 1997 BY GRAPHIS INC., 141 LEXINGTON AVENUE, NEW YORK, NY 10016 • JACKET AND BOOK DESIGN COPYRIGHT © 1997 BY PEDERSEN DESIGN • 141 LEXINGTON AVENUE, NEW YORK, NY 10016 USA NO PART OF THIS BOOK MAY BE REPRODUCED IN ANY FORM WITHOUT WRITTEN PERMISSION OF THE PUBLISHER • PRINTED IN SINGAPORE BY C.S. GRAPHICS.

IMAGES OF DUTCH POSTERS FEATURED ON PAGES 36-63 COURTESY OF THE POSTER COLLECTION OF THE MUSEUM FÜR GESTALTUNG, ZÜRICH.

OPPOSITE • DESIGN BY FRED WOODWARD / PHOTOGRAPH BY ALBERT WATSON

Massimo Vignelli

I believe design is the balance of utility and beauty. If the balance is in favor of utility, we have commercial design. If the balance is in favor of beauty, we have a work of art, something devoid of utility, as art is supposed to be. The strength of art is its independence from performing a task beyond its intellectual being. Art with purpose is commercial or propaganda–"art," with a lower case "a." To strike a balance between utility and beauty requires a strong

commitment to quality, because quality begins to appear when the balance between those two forces is reached. ✦ I believe that balance between utility and beauty is at the base even of typeface design, and typography is the structure of a message to be conveyed. Let us examine for a moment the need for new typefaces. We all know the history of typefaces, type design and how man has striven to achieve a better definition of type through technological improvements in order to obtain a clearer expression of feelings and better legibility. ✦ But we also know that throughout the last two hundred years industry has produced typefaces mainly to make profit, just like any other industry. For the most part, typefaces have been produced by greed rather than need. That continues today on a greater scale than ever. This greed has been nourished by the advertising industry which continuously demands new typefaces to provide "identity" to its clients by giving them a unique, distinctive typeface of their own. ✦ Periodically there is desire for a new typeface to replace a previous one which has been suffering from overexposure. This usually represents a desire for refinement, or a desire for a wider articulation of weights or sizes to achieve a better relationship between particular typefaces. In this category I remember the desire for a typeface with tighter letterspacing than "standard" or "new gothic" typefaces, which eventually gave birth to Helvetica or the desire for a wider articulation of weights, extended or condensed forms that gave birth to Univers. And so on from Garamond to Sabon, from Bodoni to Our Bodoni, etc. ✦ The advent of the computer as a working tool for our profession has sharpened our sensitivity and consequently our desire for a wider range of type values.

Never in the history of type have we had more control than today. Type size, kerning and line spacing have never been more controllable and adjustable than today. Nor has it ever been more possible to obtain sublime typography. But it has also never been more possible for anyone to produce the most horrible visual trash ever seen. ✦ I think with horror of young children growing up in a world where words are compressed, extended, deformed or destroyed by incompetent people playing with type. I do not mean designers (although they are often guilty of similar crimes), but the plethora of people substituting for designers. The computer has created a new level of visual pollution, to which we must respond as designers to prevent further damage. We should realize that irresponsible extensions of so-called cutting-edge designs could create a bloody mess. It should be made clear that those designs are, at their best, art pieces devoid of utilitarian use, not suitable for everyday purposes. ✦ I think that typography as an element of the organization of information should be brought back to the center of attention where it belongs, so that more articulate, more expressive, more understandable ways can be found to convey content. ✦ Typography is so rich with means proper to its own nature, that so much could be obtained to clearly express any content, and any feeling, in a way that glorifies human intellect by being useful and beautiful at the same time. ✦ Typography, like architecture, can take many forms and be either sublime or ridiculous. Like architecture, typography can be responsible or irresponsible, boring or exciting. But in the end, its life and glory depends on the proper balance between utility and beauty. Without that, typography is only trash.

MASSIMO VIGNELLI IS AN AWARD-WINNING DESIGNER WHOSE WORK HAS BEEN PUBLISHED AND EXHIBITED AROUND THE WORLD.

5TH CENTURY B.C.

Greek Lapidary Type

One of the first formal uses of western letterforms. The Greeks adopted the Phoenician alphabet for their own needs, and as a result changed several of the letters and created the foundation for western writing.

2ND CENTURY B.C.

Roman Lapidary Type

Transitional letterforms from ancient Greek to the more modern Roman shapes and proportions.

1ST CENTURY B.C.

Roman Monumental Capitals

The foundation for western type design and ancestor of all serifed typefaces.

4TH-5TH CENTURY

Square Capitals

Formal hand-written letters which evolved from the Roman Monumental Capitals.

8TH-11TH CENTURY

Carolingian minuscule

Thanks to Charlemagne, this became the basis for the standard lowercase alphabet.

14TH CENTURY

Johann Gutenberg (1394-1468)

Although he did not invent movable type, the printing press, printing ink, or was even the first person to print with metal type, Gutenberg did invent the art of typography. Gutenberg's contribution was that he took all these existing devices and synthesized them into an economical and practical product. The adjustable mold, which Gutenberg did invent, enabled one model of a letterform, produced by a designer, to be replicated thousands of times. Gutenberg then took these products and combined them into works

of typographic art that, over 500 years later, are still considered to be some of the best ever produced.

15TH CENTURY

Nicolas Jenson (1420-1480)

Jenson was one of the first printers to cut and use fonts based on Roman, rather that northern European, Fraktur letterform. Revivals of his type include William Morris' Golden Type, and the very successful Jenson Oldstyle first released by American Type Founders in 1893.

William Caxton (1421-1491)

Generally credited with introducing the craft of printing with movable type to England. He also printed one of the first commercial advertisements: a poster which extolled the products and services of his print shop. Caxton was first a successful businessman and government official, and only began his typographic career after his retirement from these earlier endeavors. The earliest fonts Caxton used were imported from mainland Europe, but when his business was established he was able to convince a noted Flemish calligrapher to change his profession to that of typeface designer, and move to England to produce fonts of type. Caxton eventually had eight fonts produced for his press, most of the Black Letter style of northern Germany. One of these is generally considered to be the ancestor of the "Old English" types that are still used today.

1450

Gutenberg Bible printed

(The birth of the art of typography)

Aldus Manutius (1450-1515)

Great Italian printer and type founder. Commissioned Francesco Griffo to design several faces, the most important of which is now

revived under the name "Bembo." The basis for the face was first used in Pietro Bembo's DeAetna, printed by Manutius in a font designed by Griffo. It is interesting to note that Griffo only designed a lowercase for the project, with the caps being pulled from an existing font. Manutius is generally credited with the invention of italic type as means to produce inexpensive books. The former is true, however, not the latter. Manutius never produced an inexpensive book in his life. The italic type was created as a "marketing tool" to help sell his books to well-off scholars and government officials who wrote in a similar style.

1476

Caxton sets up his printing business in the Almonry of Westminster Abbey.

1496

Bembo

Forerunner of the typeface Bembo is first used in Pietro Bembo's DeAetna 1495, and named for him. It was a model followed by Garamond, and the ancestor of many European types through the 17th century.

16TH CENTURY

Claude Garamond (1500-1567)

The first to sell fonts of his type to others as a business. He was the first designer to create faces, cut punches, and then sell the type produced from the punches. Unfortunately, even though many bought and used his fonts, Garamond had little lasting success in this business. In fact, when he died he owned little more than his punches, and shortly after his death his widow was forced to sell even these. Thus began the time-honored tradition of type designers creating beautiful tools for others to use profitably. (There are wealthy graphic designers, illustrators, and art directors—there are no

wealthy type designers.) On the plus side, Garamond was the most distinguished type designer of his time, perhaps of the entire Renaissance. A true typographic innovator, he was instrumental in the adoption of roman typeface designs in France as a replacement for the commonly used gothic, or black letter, fonts. He was one of the first type designers to create obliqued capitals to complement an italic lowercase.

While his designs were exceptionally popular for a very long time (sort of the Helvetica of their day) as with most typestyles, the Garamond designs did not enjoy uninterrupted popularity. After a time new French designs and styles created by English, Dutch and Italian foundries began to replace Garamond's type as the design of choice among printers. It wasn't until the beginning of the twentieth century that new versions of the Garamond style began to appear again in print shops.

Robert Granjon (1513-1589)

Active from 1545 to 1589, Robert Granjon is credited with introducing the italic form of type as a complement to the roman faces that were popular at the time. His work is closely associated with that of Claude Garamond. His work has provided the models for both Plantin and Times New Roman, as well as Matthew Carter's Galliard. The face that bears his name, however, is based on a design by Claude Garamond.

1530

Garamond's first roman type appeared in *Paraphrais* in *Elgantiarum Libros Laurentii Vallae.*

Jean Jannon (1580-1658)

The type designer who created the face on which

most modern Garamond revivals are based. Jannon worked more than 80 years after Garamond, and was the first to release revivals of the earlier Frenchman's work. Because of his religious beliefs, Jannon was continually getting into trouble with the Catholic government of France. On one such occasion his fonts were confiscated, and eventually found their way into the French National Printing Office where they remained in obscurity for over 200 years. In the twentieth century they were mistakenly used as a basis for the first revival of Garamond's type.

17TH CENTURY

William Caslon (1692-1766)

Originally an English gunsmith who became a type designer and founder of the Caslon Type Foundry. Also one of the very few type designers who was wealthy. His work was based on earlier Dutch designs, and does not possess the irreproachable perfection like that of Bodoni or Baskerville. Caslon's strength as a type designer was not in his ability to create flawless letters, but to create a font of type that when set in a block of text copy appears perfect in spite of the vagaries and individuality of each letterform.

The first modern revivals of Caslon's work were released in America under the name of "Old Style." When American Type Founders was formed in 1892, this design was later renamed "Caslon 471." The many succeeding ATF Caslons: Monotype Caslon, Adobe Caslon, and even ITC Caslon are all based on the work of William Caslon. His surviving punches are now in the St. Bride's Printing Library in London.

18TH CENTURY

John Baskerville (1706-1775)

He was cranky, vain and scornful of convention. His peers disapproved of him, his type, and his printing. Baskerville was also an iconoclast of the first order. He lived with a woman for sixteen years before marrying her (something not unheard of in 18th century England– but also not something approved by 18th century British society). He also built a mausoleum on his property to be used for his burial, because of his life-time aversion to Christianity.

Since almost no one liked Baskerville's fonts or printing, his work was truly created out of love for the craft. In the truest sense, Baskerville was an amateur. Freedom from paying customers, however, provided Baskerville with a benefit to his work: he was allowed to take as much time and be as demanding as he wanted. Whether his peers liked his work or not, few could argue that it was not perfect. Lack of paying clients also provided Baskerville the opportunity to experiment with practically every aspect of type founding and printing. His first endeavor was to create fonts of type, but Baskerville soon found that the printing technology of the day did not allow him to print with them as he wished. As a result he explored, changed, and improved virtually all aspects of the printing process. He made his own printing press, a vastly improved version over others of the day; he developed his own ink, that even today is difficult to match for darkness and richness; he invented the hot-pressing process to create smooth paper stock, and even had a small mill built on his property to produce paper that met his standards.

Today Baskerville's unpopular type is one of the most popular and most used serif typestyles. It is represented in essentially every type library, and can be reproduced on practically every kind of imaging device.

Pierre Simon Fournier (1712-1768)

French printer and type designer. His work predated Bodoni's, and is really the foundation for much of Bodoni's first typeface designs. Monotype Fournier and Barbou are based on Fournier's work, as is Dwiggins Electra.

1734

Caslon types first shown

Although based on Dutch old style weights and proportions, William Caslon's font became the first great British type and set the standard for all that followed. It is said that, just as Shakespeare gave England a national theater, Caslon give the country a national typeface.

Giambattista Bodoni (1740-1813)

The typography and type designs Bodoni created are still regarded as being among the most refined and elegant ever produced. But then, he had the luxury of almost limitless time, money, and effort to spend on his projects. Bodoni worked for the Duke of Parma, and, outside of the occasional royal commission, only worked on projects that he wanted.

Bodoni's type was the result of an evolutionary process. The first fonts he used were old style designs purchased from Fournier, and when he began to cut his own fonts, they were based heavily on the Fournier type. Over many years Bodoni's design style changed to the modern style that we are familiar with today. It is interesting to note that when his style changed, Bodoni would simply recut specific letters for existing fonts

to make them current. Bodoni, was also one of history's most prolific creators of type. He was a demanding and exacting typographer that wanted to be able to use exactly the size and proportion of type that best suited his needs. As a result he created literally hundreds of fonts–all in the Bodoni style. An 1840 inventory of his output showed over 25,000 punches and over 50,000 matrices!

1762

Baskerville typeface first used

Archetypical transitional type, John Baskerville's fonts bridged the gap between the old style designs produced in the renaissance and the moderns created by Didot and Bodoni.

19TH CENTURY

1816

First sans serif font

Designed by William Caslon IV, the great, great grand-son of the William Caslon that gave us the English serifed design. Many claim that the design for this sans is based on the Greek Lapidary letters of the 5th century. Note how close they also look to the caps found in faces like Futura, and ITC Avant Garde Gothic.

1818

Bodoni

The quintessential modern type is shown in Giambattista Bodoni's "Manuale," completed by his wife after his death. Today, there are hundreds of Bodoni revival designs based on those shown in this benchmark of typography.

1821

Italienne

Italienne, one of the first commercially popular advertising display designs is first used. Because serifs

are heavier than main character strokes, this style of type has been called a "reversed Egyptian."

1844

Clarendon

Clarendon is first released Originally released by R Besley & Co. Type Founders in England, as a heavy face to accompany standard text composition in directories and dictionaries. The face became popular as an advertising display face and was copied by other foundries.

Frederic Goudy (1865-1947)

One of America's most prolific and well-known type designers. As a type designer Goudy displayed originality and technical skill. He created more, and more diverse, typefaces than any designer before him. (Morris Fuller Benton may have created a larger and more divergent library, but he had a staff of designers to help him with his task.) As a designer and printer Goudy developed a distinctive personal style. Early on he learned that even the most beautiful typefaces were doomed to failure, without a good marketing program. As a result, Goudy used his faces in specimen books and promotional material that were both exceptional graphic designs and compelling marketing vehicles. In addition, Goudy was his own best spokesperson.

It is a testimony to Goudy's ability that so many of his designs are still in active use. Kennerly is available from a wide variety of sources. Goudy Old Style is a modern classic. Italian Old Style, National Old /style, Garamont, Deepdene, and even Goudy Sans are available as state-of-the-art digital fonts. Copperplate Gothic, which was an ATF best seller in fonts of metal, is also a Goudy design.

And finally, ITC Berkeley Oldstyle is a revival of Goudy's University of California Old Style.

Goudy's achievements are even more remarkable in that he was self-taught, and did not begin to make his first designs until the age of 30.

Morris Fuller Benton (1872-1948)

The unknown father of American type design. The person behind American Type Founders type development program for over 35 years. Along with Fred Goudy and Ed Benguiat, one of America's most prolific type designers. Benton is responsible for novelty designs such as Broadway, Tower and Wedding Text, sans serifs such as Alternate Gothic, Franklin Gothic and News Gothic, Mainstay advertising faces like Century Oldstyle, Stymie, and the Cheltenham family. He also created the first modern revival of Bodoni's work, and developed the quintessential legibility face in Century Schoolbook–and this is only a sampling of his prodigious work. For many years ATF had the greatest offering of typefaces in the world–Morris Fuller Benton essentially built this offering.

Emil Rudolf Weiss (1875-1943)

A leading German typographer, designer, and calligrapher, Emil Weiss was associated with the Bauer foundry in the 30's and 40's. His best-known design is the Memphis family of type.

Rudolf Koch (1876-1934)

Koch was primarily a calligrapher and teacher, but his association with the Klingspor type foundry in Germany provided the opportunity for a number his designs to be made into fonts of type. Most famous for his sans serif design, Cable, he is also responsible for several other typefaces that have been made into fonts of digital type. His calligraphic Locarno has been enlarged into a much bigger family than he anticipated, and Neuland is available from several sources. Other faces by Koch include: Holla, Jessen, Marathon, Offenbach Steel and Wallau.

Lucian Bernhard (1885-1972)

Lucian Bernhard was a character. He never owned an automobile, radio, television, or virtually any other electrical appliance. He was an avid tango dancer and a world-class admirer (our enlightened society might use harsher words) of women. He was also fond of telling tails about himself (like how he ran away from home because he was hopelessly in love with the bareback rider) that were charming – but he probably stretched the truth more than a little.

Bernhard began designing typefaces as a young man in Germany. His first was cut in 1910. From then on he designed a typeface a year until he came to America in 1922 to work with American Type Founders, for which he produced 13 types. Many of his typefaces are still available, among them: Bernhard Cursive, Bernhard Gothic, Bernhard Tango, and Bernhard Fashion. Unfortunately, a few such as Bernhard Booklet, Bernhard Brushscript, and Lucian are not available today.

Paul Renner (1878-1956)

Creator of the first modern, geometric sans serif face: Futura. Although not a member of the Bauhaus, Renner shared its ideals and believed that a modern typeface should express modern models, rather than be revivals of previous designs. His original renderings for Futura's lowercase were much more experiential and geometric in character than those which were finally released by the Bauer foundry.

Oswald Cooper (1879-1940)

Primarily a lettering artist and graphic designer, Oswald Cooper is also responsible for designing a number of advertising display typefaces. All his type designs are patterned after his hand lettering. A student of Frederick Goudy, Cooper shunned the limelight, becoming famous in his time almost in spite of himself. As his fame in graphic arts, copy writing, and advertising spread, he was approached by the Barnhart Bros. foundry to produce his own type designs. Creating over a dozen families of type, Cooper persisted in thinking of himself as "just" a lettering artist.

His most well-known typeface, Cooper Black, started the 20th century trend for ultra bold typefaces and has been called a "design for farsighted printers and nearsighted readers." Recently there has been a revival of several of his designs, the more important of which are Oz Handicraft from Bitstream and ITC Ozwald and ITC Highlander from International Typeface Corporation.

William Addison Dwiggins (1880-1956)

American graphic, typographic, and book designer. Dwiggins also designed the typefaces Caledonia, Eldorado, Electra, Falcon, and Metro for Mergenthaler Linotype. Dwiggins' self imposed challenge in all his type designs was to create beautiful and utilitarian typefaces for machine composition. In fact, it was this challenge that was the catalyst for Dwiggins to begin his career in type design. He once wrote an article in the trade press complaining that there were no acceptable gothic typefaces available for Linotype composition. Upon seeing the article, Chauncey Griffith, the Director of Typography at Mergenthaler Linotype,

wrote Dwiggins a letter which, in essence, said, "If you think you're so good. lets see the gothic you can draw." The challenge was accepted and thus began the 27 year association between Mergenthaler Linotype and William Dwiggins.

Eric Gill (1882-1940)

English sculptor, stone cutter, artist and type designer. His most important work, and his only sans, is Gill Sans. Other designs include Joanna, Perpetua and Pilgrim. A true iconoclast, Gill is also well known for his radical political beliefs, and sexual adventures.

It was through his friendship with Stanley Morison and Beatrice Warde that Gill first began to design type. His first face, Perpetua, was commissioned by Morison because he felt that Gill's background in stone cutting would give him an understanding of the construction and purpose of serifs. Gill Sans was also designed at the request of Morison. The design goal for Gill Sans was to provide Monotype with an alternative design to the many geometric sans serif faces being released in Europe at the same time. While not a geometric design like its competition, Gill's sans became the most popular serifless type in England.

Victor Hammer (1882-1967)

Type designer Victor Hammer created American Uncial, his most famous design, in 1943. Born in Australia, Hammer acquired a reputation for craftsmanship as a designer, punchcutter, and printer in Italy. He immigrated to the U.S. and became a professor of fine arts at Wells College in Aurora, New York in 1939, where he cut the punches for Uncial.

Stanley Morison (1889-1967)

Though not a type designer, lettering artist, or calligrapher, Stanley Morison was one of the most influential figures in modern British typography. As Typographical Advisor to the Monotype Corporation for over 25 years, he was responsible for the release of such classic designs as Rockwell, Gill Sans, Perpetua, Albertus, and perhaps his most successful face Times New Roman. In addition to new type styles, Morison also sponsored a series of typeface revivals that was unequaled in Britain or Europe. Monotype's revival of Bembo, Baskerville, Ehrhardt, Fournier, and Walbaum are just a part of Morison's typographic contribution.

Although rarely referenced in books on typographic history, another one of Morison's contributions to the communications arts was his avid support of Beatrice Warde. Morison was Warde's friend, lover, and, perhaps most important, mentor. Morison provided Warde with the opportunity and guidance to excel as a typographic historian, publicist, and passionate advocate for the printing arts.

1892

American Type Founders

Founded as a consortium of 23 individual type foundries. In the late 1800s the demand for type was intense, but because there were so many competing type foundries, each having to design, manufacture, market and distribute their own fonts, the business of type was in a turmoil. ATF was founded as a venture to improve business margins and restore stability to the type industry. Not only were the consortium's commercial goals met, the design community benefited from the monumental outpouring of exceptional

type designs it produced. In its most prolific years between 1900 and 1935, ATF build the foundation of American type design.

Jan Van Krimpen (1892-1957)

A good type designer and one of the greatest book typographers of the twentieth century. His first, and most successful type design was Lutetia, which he drew for the prestigious printing house of Enschedé en Zonen in the Netherlands. Other faces by Van Krimpen are Cancelleresca Bastarda, Romanée, Romulus, Spectrum and Van Dijck.

Georg Trump (1895-1985)

A teacher of graphic design and type designer primarily associated with the Weber foundry in Germany. His most important design was Trump Mediaeval was released in 1954. He also drew the typefaces City, Delphin, Schadow Antiqua, and Codex.

Charles Peignot (1897-1983)

Director of Deberny & Peignot for nearly 50 years, Charles Peignot was closely involved with the creation of all new faces emanating from his foundry. He commissioned the poster artist A.M. Cassandre to create the typeface that bears his name, Peignot. He was at the forefront in the cause for typeface copyright protection and helped found the Association Typographique International.

1898

Akzidenz Grotesk released

The great, great grandparent of Helvetica, first issued by Berthold. It provided yeoman duty as, what was then called, a "jobbing face" for many years until it was replaced by the geometric sans serif designs of the 1930s. Revival of Akzidenz Grotesk came at the hands of Max Miedinger in 1957.

Robert Hunter Middleton (1898-1985)
Type Director for Ludlow type foundry for almost 50 years years. He devoted his entire professional life to the Ludlow company. By the time he retired, Middleton had created almost 100 typefaces, among them Radiant, Stellar, Karnak and Record Gothic.

20TH CENTURY

1900

Century Expanded
In 1894, the Century type was cut by Linn Boyd Benton in collaboration with Theodore Low DeVinne for the Century Magazine. The objective was a darker, more readable typeface than the type that was currently being used. It was also somewhat condensed to accommodate the magazine's two-column format. Century Expanded, drawn by Morris Fuller Benton, is a wider version of the magazine typeface.

Max Miedinger (circa 1900-1980)
In the 1950s, under the direction of Edouard Hoffmann, Max Miedinge of Zurich, Switzerland was asked to update Haas Grotesk, a version of Berthold's Akzidenz Grotesk, for the Haas foundry. His creation, New Haas Grotesque, was rechristened Helvetica, the typeface that has supplanted Futura as the most widely used typeface in the world.

Beatrice Warde (1900-1969)
Although she never drew a typeface, she was one of the most important women in modern typographic history. Warde was the passion behind the typographical efforts of Monotype during its most important years from 1925 into the 1950s. More than once she has been called the "First Lady of Typography." Beatrice Warde was Monotype's director of publicity, but she did not limit her

influence to simple marketing programs. She was an educator, historian, typographer, and the moving force behind Eric Gill's design of Gill Sans and Perpetua.

Jan Tschichold (1902-1974)
In the early part of this century, Jan Tschichold revolutionized typography by virtually single-handedly making asymmetric typographic arrangement the style of choice among young designers. For many years, Tschichold created posters, book covers, advertisements and even letterheads which were quintessential examples of asymmetric design. His work not only created a new typographic genre, it also served as the benchmark of those who followed in his footsteps.

In addition to being a teacher, typographer, book designer, and rebel, Tschichold was also a typeface designer. Sabon, a typographic tour de force, is the face which establishes Tschichold's reputation as a type designer.

1903

Franklin Gothic released by American Type Founders

Warren Chappell (1904-1991)
American type designer and typographic scholar. Chappell studied under Rudolf Koch in Germany and created typefaces for both American and European foundries. His works include: Trajanus, Lydian and Lydian Cursive.

1904

Franklin Gothic released
Named after Benjamin Franklin and originally issued in just one weight, the Franklin Gothic family was expanded over the years to include several designs.

1906

Century Oldstyle released
Morris Fuller Benton's "old style" addition to the Century family. An exceptionally successful melding of Century typeface and old style design traits. Although almost 90 years old, still one of he most used serif designs for advertising typography.

Roger Excoffon (1910-1983)
French graphic and type designer who created, among other faces, Mistral in 1953 and Antique Olive in the 1960s. Antique Olive has always been popular in its country of origin, but did not enjoy success outside of France until Compugraphic Corporation (now Agfa Miles) released, and heavily promoted the face in the late 1970s.

1915

Century Schoolbook released
This design was a result of Morris Fuller Benton's research into vision and reading comprehension. It was conceived and widely used for setting of children's schoolbooks. the face also served as the foundation for the many "legibility" types that followed.

1915

Goudy Oldstyle released
Although he was not totally satisfied with the design, the most consistently popular of Fred Goudy's many typefaces.

Tony Stan (1917-1988)
A prolific contemporary New York letter and type designer affiliated with PhotoLettering Inc, and International Typeface Corporation, Tony Stan has created and/or adapted a number of typefaces to create such designs as ITC Berkeley Old Style, ITC Garamond, ITC Century, and ITC Cheltenham.

1917

First modern revival of Garamond released by American Type Founders.

Freeman (Jerry) Craw (1917-)
American graphic and type designer of both metal and phototype faces, among them Craw Clarendon, Craw Modern and Ad Lib. For several years he was vice president and art director of Tri-Arts Press during which time he was responsible for some of the most eloquent printed material produced in America.

Herb Lubalin (1918-1981)
American graphic and typographic designer. In the 1960s and 1970s his graphic design and typographic handling broke new ground for creativity and at the same time set the standard for graphic communication that was emulated by much of the graphic design community. He was a designer of logotypes, posters, magazines, advertising, packaging, books, stationery, and collateral promotional materials. In addition, Lubalin was one of the founders of ITC, and the creator of more than 200 alphabets. He was responsible for such typefaces as ITC Lubalin Graph, Busorama, and ITC Ronda, and was the co-designer, along with Tom Carnese, of ITC Avant Garde Gothic.

Hermann Zapf (1918-)
One of the 20th century's most important and prolific typeface designers, Hermann Zapf has created such universally acclaimed typefaces as Optima, Palatino, Melior, ITC Zapf Chancery, and ITC Zapf Dingbats. He began his career with the Stempel foundry in West Germany after the war. Since leaving Stempel in 1956, Zapf has created typefaces for foundries such as Berthold,

Linotype, and ITC, in addition to many exclusive designs for private and corporate use. Zapf is also probably the world's most famous and successful calligrapher.

Aldo Novarese (1920-1995)
Italian type designer responsible for a variety of text and display designs. Early in his career he was associated with the Nebiolo type foundry in Turin and created faces primarily in conjunction with Alessandro Butti, among them Augustea and Microgramma (which later became Eurostile when he added a lowercase). Later in his career Novarese developed several faces which became ITC designs. His most successful being ITC Novarese. Others are ITC Symbol and ITC Mixage.

Aaron Burns (1922-1991)
Typographer and founder of International Typeface Corporation. Although not a type designer, Burns contribution to the typographic is as significant as many of the most important and well known creators of typefaces. Over 600 original and revival typeface designs have been released and many type designers were provided a first opportunity to create a commercial typeface design as a result of the company Burns founded.

1927

Kabel released
Named for the Transatlantic Cable, Rudolph Koch designed this geometric sans for the Klingspor type foundry.

Ed Benguiat (1927-)
Benguiat has drawn over 600 typefaces, possibly more than any other type designer. He has designed faces for International Typeface Corporation, for PhotoLettering Inc., and for a variety of

corporate clients. He has created revivals of old metal faces such as ITC Souvenir, ITC Bookman, and Sara Bernhardt. He has drawn absolutely new, and original designs such as Charisma, ITC Panache, and Spectra. Benguiat has not only designed more faces than Benton, Goudy, Zapf, and Frutiger, he may have created more type than all these designers combined.

1928

Gill Sans released
Commissioned by Stanley Morison for Monotype, this Eric Gill design was intended to recover sales being lost to the new German geometric sans. Gill is not, however, a true geometric face in that most of its character designs and proportions are derived from classical serif designs.

Adrian Frutiger (1928-)
A contemporary Swiss graphic designer and typographer, Adrian Frutiger is one of the most important type designers of the post-World War period. He began his work as an apprentice to a printer and studied wood cutting and calligraphy before launching his career as a type designer. He was asked by Deberny and Peignot to adapt Futura, but finding it too geometric, chose instead to create a large type family with matching weights; thus, Univers was born. He has created a number of other popular type-faces—Egyptienne, Serifa, OCR-B, and the face chosen for use at the De Gaulle Airport in Roissy, France, now known as Frutiger.

1929

Futura released
Drawn by Paul Renner, this was the first modern geometric sans influenced by the Universal typeface drawn by Herbert Bayer and the Bauhaus design philosophy. Futura

became the benchmark design for a "modern" sans, forcing virtually every type foundry to create their own version.

1929

Bembo released
The 20th century version of a typeface designed by Francesco Griffo for Aldus Manutius. Monotype released the design as part of Stanley Morison's typeface revival program. Today, Bembo is available from a variety of type suppliers.

1929

Memphis
The first 20th century slab serif design is released by the Stempel Type Foundry. The similarities between this and Futura are obvious. Almost all type suppliers now have their slab serif version of Memphis, and many completely original designs, as a result of this font's success.

1930

Metro released
The only sans serif type designed by William Dwiggins. Although original-ly intended for newspaper headline copy, this face has become popular for a variety of advertising display applications. A face with more humanity than Helvetica or Univers, less obvious overtones than Gill Sans, and just a hint of art deco panache, Metro is unlike most other sans.

1932

Times Roman released
Commissioned by The Times of London newspaper. Stanley Morison supervised the design and provided the original Plantin specimens used to draw the face. The designer, Victor Lardent, an artist on the Times staff, was appointed by Morison.

Friedrich Poppl (1932-1982)
German type designer who worked primarily for the

Berthold Type Foundry. His faces are best known in Europe; among them are Poppl-Pontiflex and Poppl-Laudatio.

Leslie Usherwood (1932-1983)
Leslie Usherwood began his career as a lettering artist in the field of commercial art. He founded Typesettra, Ltd. in Toronto in 1968. The creator of Caxton, ITC Usherwood, and Flange, he specialized in hand lettering and headline typefaces.

Matthew Carter (1937-)
The son of printing historian Harry Carter, Matthew Carter can be considered one of the founders of electronic type. The designer of Bell Centennial for Linotype and ITC Galliard with Mike Parker, he and Parker founded Bitstream in 1981 to design and market type in digital form. Bitstream Charter is the first of his new designs. Currently working on new designs, he is the founder and principal designer of Carter & Cone Type, Inc. Carter is also a charter member of the "Type Mafia." (see "1980" for explanation of the Type Mafia)

1938

Radiant released
Stressed sans released by Ludlow. It was intended to express the modern spirit of the 1940s while breaking away from previous sans serifs geometric proportions and monotone weight.

1938

Caledonia released
by Mergenthaler Linotype

Tom Carnese (1939-)
Best known for his collaborations with Herb Lubalin at ITC, Tom Carnese has created or helped to create a number of popular fonts, including ITC Avant Garde Gothic, ITC Bolt Bold, and ITC Pioneer.

Gerard Unger (1942-)
Dutch type designer who has drawn several faces for the Enschedé type foundry in the Netherlands and Dr-Inf Rudolf Hell in Germany. Also drew Amerigo for Bitstream.

Dave Farey (1943-)
British type designer who grew out of the "Letraset" school. Designed faces such as ITC Beesknees, ITC Ozwald, ITC Highlander, Aries, ITC Golden Cockerel, and the Creative Alliance revival of Stellar.

Colin Brignall (1945-)
British type designer and director of type develop-ment at Letraset. Although originally created for dry-transfer lettering, many of his faces have become standards of photo and digital typogra-phy. Some of his more important designs are Corinthian, Edwardian, Italia, Revue, Romic and most recently, Retro. Member of the "Type Mafia"

Allan Haley (1945-)
Not a designer, but proba-bly responsible for the release of more typefaces than any other single per-son. Built the Compugraphic phototype library, the ITC typeface library from 1982-1993, and the Creative Alliance type library. Chronicler of the type design community. Some say, founder of the "Type Mafia."

Sumner Stone (1945-)
American type designer and former director of typographic development for Adobe Systems. His most important design to date has been the ITC Stone family of type, the series of serif, sans serif, and informal alphabets have common weights and proportions. Stone is also a Member of the "Type Mafia"

David Quay (1947-)
British type designer who drew ITC Quay Sans, and more recently Coptek, La Bamba and Lambada for Letraset.

Erik Spiekermann (1947-)
German type and graphic designer. Member of the "Type Mafia." Spiekermann has designed faces such as ITC Officina, Lo Type, and Berliner Grotesk for Berthold, and is one of the principals of Meta Design.

1948

Trade Gothic released
by Mergenthaler Linotype

Kris Holmes (1950-)
American type designer who has designed typefaces for Compugraphic Corporation, and Dr-Inf Rudolf Hell in Germany. Some of her designs include ITC Isadora, Shannon (which she designed in conjunction with Janice Prescott), and Lucida (which she worked on with her business partner, Charles Bigelow)

1950

Palatino released
by Mergenthaler Linotype.

1954

The first phototypesetting machine placed in a commercial business.

1954

Trump Mediaeval Released

David Berlow (1955-)
American type designer and proprietor of the Font Bureau, one of America's most prolific and creative type supply companies. Prior to opening the Font Bureau he was a type designer for Bitstream Inc. and Mergenthaler Linotype. Member of the "Type Mafia."

Cynthia Hollandsworth (1955-)

Type designer and advocate for the protection of designer's rights. Her faces include Hiroshige, ITC Tiepolo, and Wile Roman. In 1987 she formed the Typeface Design Coalition, an association of type foundries and type designers whose common goal is the protection of typeface designs. Member of the "Type Mafia"

Robert Slimbach (1956-)

American type designer who worked as a letter designer for Autologic, then as a freelance designer before joining Adobe Systems in 1987. Creator of ITC Slimbach, ITC Giovanni, Adobe Garamond, Utopia, Minion, Poetica, Adobe Jenson, Kepler and several other faces.

1957

Helvetica released

Max Miedinger's revival of Akzidenz Grotesk. First released as New Haas Grotesk, the design was later changed to its present name in honor of its country of origin: Helvetica (Switzerland). Miedinger's first release only three variants, other styles and weights were added over many years and by several designers. If you are looking for design continuity, try Neue Helvetica.

1958

Optima released

Hermann Zapf's favorite typeface. (He used it to set his own wedding invitation.) While not the first, Optima has become the benchmark for all stressed, or calligraphic, sans serif typefaces. Optima italic was also one of the first typefaces to be created through the aid of mechanical distortion system. The roman was photographically obliqued as a starting point for the design, by the New York typography studio of PhotoLettering Inc.

Carol Twombly (1959-)

A graduate of the Rhode Island School of Design and Stanford University. Ms. Twombly has worked at Bitstream and Adobe Systems. Designs to her credit are Mirarae (which won the Morisawa Typeface Design Competition in 1984), Charlemagne, Lithos, Trajan, and Viva, Nueva and many other designs.

Zuzana Licko (1961-)

Czechoslovakian designer who emigrated to the United States in 1968. Licko first created type designs to be used in the publication Emigré, but because they were met with so much enthusiasm by the young design community, the faces were eventually made into commercial fonts. Her more successful faces are Matrix, and Variex.

1962

Eurostile released

Square sans first released as a cap only face from the Nebiolo Foundry. Later Aldo Novarese drew lowercase characters to complement the earlier designs he collaborated on with A. Butti, and the face was reissued and renamed Microgramma.

1966

Sabon released

Roman type designed by Jan Tschichold. Important because it was the result of a joint design program on the part of Linotype Stempel and Monotype to create a face that was concurrently available as hand-set and machine-set metal type as well as photo type fonts. The roman is based on a Garamond design and the italic on a Granjon font.

1968

Compugraphic Corporation

The company that made low cost phototypesetting a practical reality, entered the phototypesetting machinery market.

1969

International Typeface Corporation

Founded as a partnership of Lubalin, Burns and PhotoLettering Inc. The idea was that Herb Lubalin and Aaron Burns would provide new typeface designs and the marketing to make them successful, while PhotoLettering Inc. would supply the technical know-how to produce artwork that would serve as production tools for phototype font development. ITC is a company which some hail as "The most creative and influential type foundry since ATF," and others deride as the "MacDonald's" of typeface development. Both opinions may be correct.

1970

ITC Avant Garde Gothic released

First typeface released by International Typeface Corporation. Initially drawn by Herb Lubalin as the logo and headline face for "Avant Garde" magazine. The design was later converted to a text and display font with help of PhotoLettering Inc. in New York. Look at the caps in this face, now go back and look at the 5th century B.C. Greek lapidary type.

1970

ITC Souvenir released

The typeface designers love to hate was released. Originally developed by Morris Fuller Benton for ATF in 1918, Ed Benguiat revived the basic design, enlarged the family and created the first italic variants. It may be the "Happy Face" of type, but it sure did sell well for many years.

1974

ITC Korinna Released

Based on a turn of the century Berthold design, but updated and revived by Ed Benguiat

1978

ITC Galliard released

Designed by Matthew Carter for Linotype, but later licensed to International typeface Corporation in 1982. Based on a sixteenth century design by Robert Granjon.

1980

Arbitrary date set for the founding of the "Type Mafia". Because of computer technology, fax machines, e-mail, and international design projects, the type design community is able to be in closer contact than ever before. The Type Mafia is a close knit, but informal group of friends and business associates who are the real power behind modern typeface design. Not all members of the organization are listed.

Max Miedinger, designer of Helvetica, dies.

1983

Adobe PostScript announced

One of the three most important technological advancements in typographic history. The first being Gutenberg's invention of the adjustable mold, and the second the Higonnet-Moyroud phototypesetting machine.

1983

ITC Berkeley Old Style released

International Typeface Corporation's revival of Goudy's University of California Oldstyle. Most popular of ITC's second series of typeface releases.

1985

Apple introduces the Macintosh and the Laser-Writer printer. Aldus releases PageMaker 1.0, and Paul Brainard coins the term "Desk TopPublishing." The rest is history.

1990

Tekton released

Possibly the "ITC Souvenir" of the 1990s. Designed by

David Siegel for Adobe Systems. Based on the hand lettering of D.K. Ching, a Seattle architect. Bodega, by Greg Thompson, is also released and proves to have a longer popular life-span than Tekton.

1992

First Adobe Multiple Masters font released.

Multiple Master technology enables the type designer to create master designs at each end of one, or more, predetermined design axes. The graphic designer can then interpolate, or generate intermediate variations, between the master designs on demand.

1993

Apple announces TrueType GX

GX fonts are heralded as "smart fonts" that can automatically insert ligatures, alternate character and swash letters, in addition to providing the graphic designer with automatic optical alignment and other typographic refinements. Unfortunately, because Apple didn't support them, Adobe didn't like them, and nobody could afford to make them, TrueType GX fonts never became popular.

1994

Nueva, a design by Carol Twombly, released by Adobe.

1995

Agfa forms the Creative Alliance with more than 30 independent type designers and type suppliers.

1996

Agfa and Monotype announce the joint production of the Creative Alliance CD. Microsoft releases Word™ '97 with more than 150 typefaces bundled for free. Berthold declares bankruptcy and Linotype-Hell is purchased by Heidelberg. Adobe Jenson is released.

Bradbury Thompson dies.

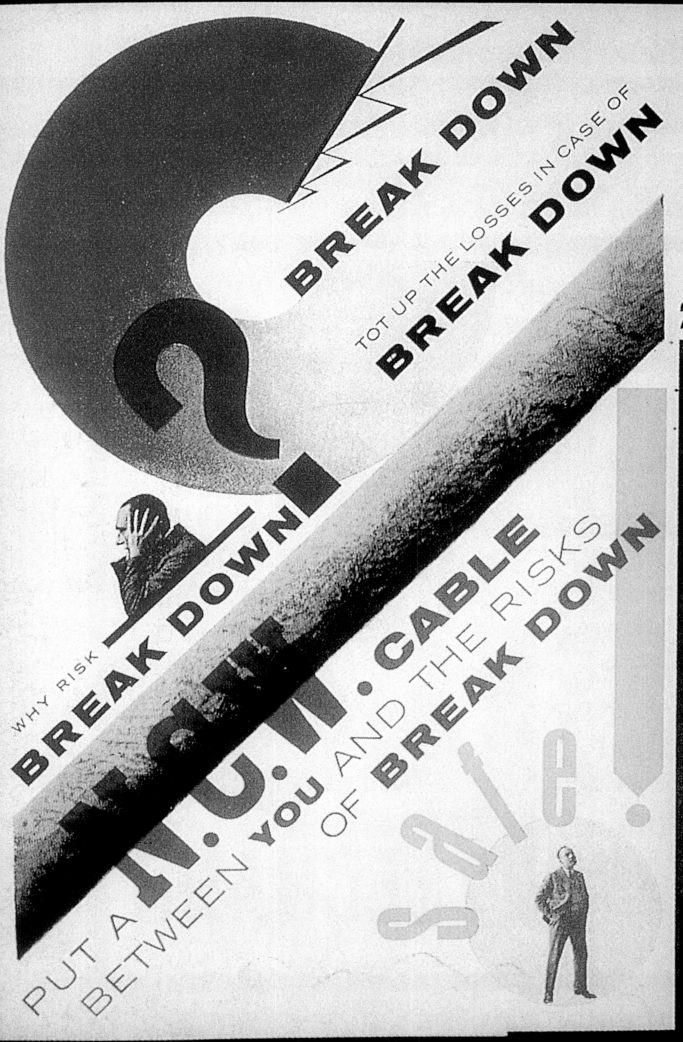

BREAK DOWN

BREAK DOWN

TOT UP THE LOSSES IN CASE OF

BREAK DOWN

25

WHY RISK

BREAK DOWN

N.G.W. CABLE

PUT A BETWEEN YOU AND THE RISKS OF BREAK DOWN

sale!

COMMENTARY

DUTCH MASTERS

Friedrich Friedl

A close look at 20th century design shows that the dominant impulses driving creative developments have emerged from contradictory attitudes. Bipolar concepts such as spontaneity and rationality, reduction and expansiveness, objectivity and abstraction have, over time, combined to give the creative process new impetus. ✧ This has been particularly true with design in the Netherlands. The country can boast many impressive examples, its designers repeatedly coming up with works which combine freedom and formal vision and lead to new developments in the world of international style. ✧ One of the first radical manifestations of the modern age was the De Stijl group. Between 1917 and 1931, a host of painters, architects and typographers (Cesar Domela, Theo van Doesburg, Vilmos Huszar, Bart van der Leck, Piet Mondrian and Piet Zwart) created a new design language, in terms of both form and content. Their creative activity was driven by the urge to reduce things to the bare essentials.

FRIEDRICH FREIDL IS A PROFESSOR OF DESIGN AND TYPOGRAPHY AT THE HOCHSCHULE FÜR GESTALTUNG IN OFFENBACH AM MAIN IN GERMANY. OPPOSITE: PORTRAIT OF FRIEERICH FRIEDL BY NORBERT MIGULETZ. PREVIOUS SPREAD: DESIGN BY PIET ZWART. (C)1998 ARTISTS RIGHTS SOCIETY (ARS), NEW YORK/BEELDRECHT, AMSTERDAM.

Avant-gardists active in the field included Paul Schuitema, Dick Elfers, Wim Brusse, Cas Corthuys, Henny Cahn, Hendrik Nicolaas Werman and Willem Sandberg among many others. Not only did they create independent designs both individually and collectively, but they were responsible for many commissioned works for cultural organisations and commercial clients alike. With their bold experiments combining photography and typography and featuring constructivist alphabets and avant-garde hand-pressed prints, they enriched the classically-oriented typography ubiquitous at the time. ✧ Covers of the magazine *Wendingen*, published between 1918 and 1931, reveal the stylistic variety of the time. Abstract and elemental forms representative of the new era soon joined the ornamental and expressive gestures which had characterized Art Nouveau and Symbolism. ✧ Until 1943, Dutch design made its own contributions to the modern age. German occupation and suppression put an abrupt stop to this creativity, but it was only a temporary hiatus. After World War II, the Dutch picked up the pieces and continued where they had left off, their identity intact. An important step was the appointment of Willem Sandberg as director of the Stedelijk Museum in Amsterdam. Already a champion of the new typography before the war, he embraced innovation and experimentation in a series of exhibitions and in his own design work. This was to have a great influence on the next generation. One need only think of Otje Oxenaar's banknote designs, Wim Crouwel's posters and "Total Design" studio, Juriaan Schrofer's typographic fantasias and Dick Dooijes and Pieter Brattinga's book on the history of the Dutch poster. The Netherlands was once again contributing remarkable figures to the international scene. ✧ The Netherlands also contributed the typographical concepts which rejuvenated Functionalism and lead it out of crisis in the 1970s. These were incredible designs, rich and overflowing with ideas, fusing references from the modern age with original forms to create a new type of multistylistic design. Gert Dumbar experimented with photography and works of graphical alienation, the "Hard Werken" group (including, among others, Gerard Hadders, Rick Vermeulen and Willem Kars) married underground and pop art to create bizarre and imaginative original works, while Anton Beeke's freethinking visualizations gave the world of posters new food for thought. There seemed to be no limit to the wealth of bold graphic forms and imaginative typographic symbols produced at the time. ✧ It was against this backdrop that the contemporary scene arose. In earlier years, designers had experimented with classical techniques; since the 1980s they have played with new media. Computers have made it much easier to create new forms for use in typographic design. However, unlike any other country, the Netherlands somehow manages not to exacerbate the generation conflict. Rather, courageous institutions, influential competitions and far-sighted jurors all play their part in ensuring that bureaucracy and dogmatism do not obstruct innovation. Although the new generation is familiar with the history of design, and although it has its models and knows how to appreciate them, it still manages to brush these models off in a friendly sort of way. Everywhere you look you will see authentic, fresh and untrammeled typographic design. Work commissioned for public institutions has provided a platform for Irma Boom, Wigger Bierma and the Wild Plakken group. The H. N. Werkman Prize and the Charles Nypels Prize have been awarded to designers such as Karel Martens, Walter Nikkels and Max Kisman. The Dutch Post Office, the financial authorities and the railways are well-known internationally and are envied for their constant formal innovation. ✧ Along with traditional specialties such as corporate identity, and book and poster design, typography has always enjoyed a special standing in the Netherlands. The *De Stijl* group's Utopian alphabets (which gave us our first hint of the computer age) were followed by Wim Crouwel's early experimental sketches for a new alphabet, which provoked international astonishment and debate. Teacher and practitioner Gerrot Noordzij trains numerous type designers who go on to achieve great success in their field. Typefaces by Bram de Does, Martin Majoor and Gerard Unger are among the most exciting and widely-used anywhere in the world. In their studio, Letterror, Erik van Blokland and Just van Rossum have designed a constantly changing typeface. What started out as a Gothic mindgame made possible by computers resulted in "Beowulf", a serious typeface which gives an idea of what creative experts will develop in future. ✧ How is it that one country can consistently produce such original typography for so long? Not only is the search for innovative and interesting new forms accepted by people and institutions commissioning work in the Netherlands, but designers manage to meet the challenge. Innovation is actively embraced and aggressively promoted by far-sighted teachers in Dutch schools. Schools in Rotterdam, The Hague, Breda, Enschede, Amsterdam, Arnhem and Maastricht all have their own specialities and turn out talented graduates and teachers. They specialize in a wide range of areas including typeface design, graphic design, experimental or socially critical forms, and the fine arts. ✧ Schools in the Netherlands all insist on teaching the basics of form and the essential skills of the trade. They encourage their students to question what they are taught, to elaborate upon it or reject it and to augment it with new technical developments. This combination of tradition and emancipation, an abundance of creative talent and the fact that many influential people and institutions accept and understand design, may explain the free and experimental development of graphic and typographic design in the Netherlands. It may also explain why the rest of the world holds the country's design in such high esteem.

Art Directors/Designers: B. Bijvoet, J. Duiker

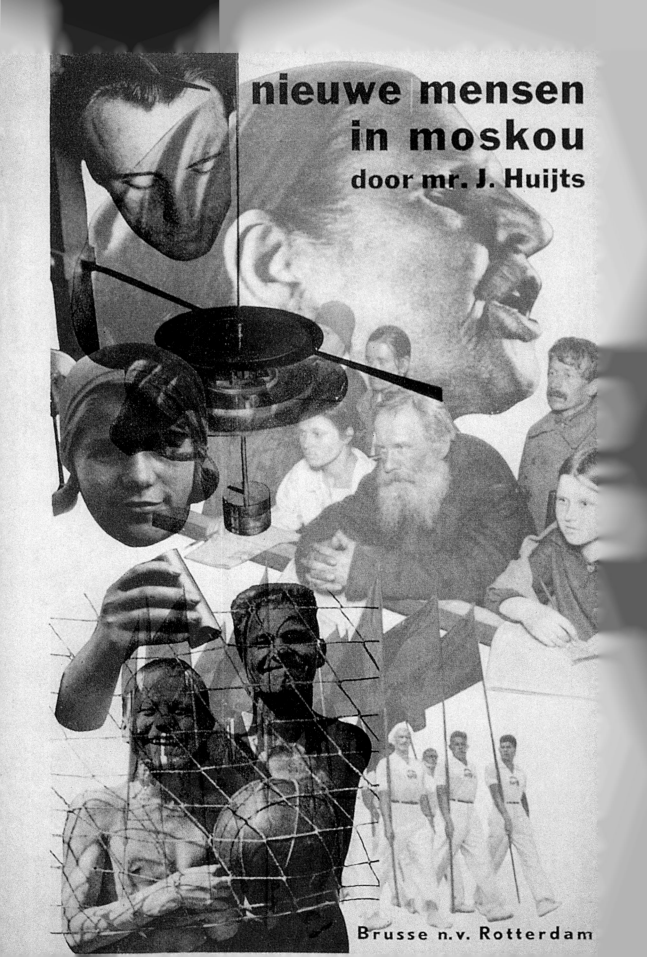

nieuwe mensen
in moskou
door mr. J. Huijts

Brusse n.v. Rotterdam

Art Director/Designer: Max Kisman

ZUKUNFT

FUTURE

PROGRESS

D   C
B
A
E
F
G
H
I
J
K
L
M   N   O   P   Q   R

Z
Y
X
W
V   U
T

ZANDERS

Papiergeschichten
Paper stories
Histoires de papier

Poster
4

Das vierte Kapitel führt in jene Welt, die man Zukunft nennt. Ein weiser Mann offenbart den papiernen Schönheiten weiteres Schicksal. Es gilt, die schönen Dinge der Welt zu erhalten. Deshalb wird die Zukunft nicht mehr sein als ein neues Kapitel einer unendlichen Geschichte. Und so wird man sich irgendwann die Fortsetzung erzählen von der Geschichte vom papiernen Schönheit, die vor langer Zeit begann, um niemals zu enden.

The fourth chapter takes us into the world we call Future. A wise man reveals the destiny of the paper white horse – to preserve the beautiful things of the world. That is why the Future is only one more chapter in his endless story. And so the continuation of the paper white horse's story will be told – a story that began a long time ago and will never end.

Le quatrième chapitre nous introduit dans le monde de l'avenir. Un sage nous invite au sort qui attend le cheval couleur de papier. Il importe de conserver leur beauté aux choses de ce monde. L'avenir ne sera donc qu'un nouveau chapitre de son histoire éternelle. C'est ainsi qu'un pourra, un jour, raconter la suite de l'histoire du cheval couleur de papier, commencée en des temps anciens pour ne jamais finir.

Art Director/Designer: Paul Schuitema
Year: ca. 1927

Art Director/Designer: Paul Schuitema
Year: 1929

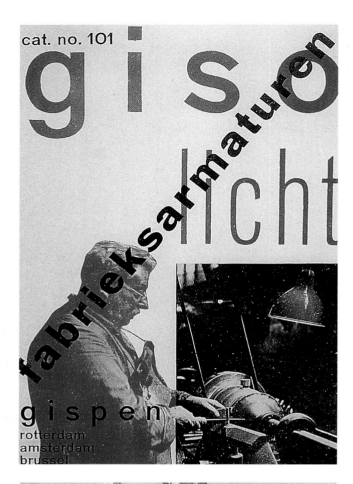

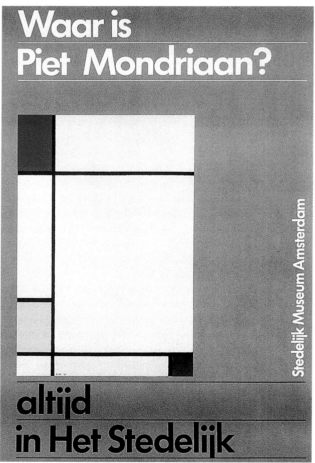

(Top left) *Art Director/Designer:* Paul Schuitema (Top right) *Art Director/Designer:* Paul Schuitema
(Bottom left) *Art Director/Designer:* Henny Cahn *Year:* 1938 (Bottom right) *Art Director/Designer:* Wim Crouwel

zomertentoonstelling

1800 – 1940

stedelijk museum amsterdam

de verzameling

nieuwe aanwinsten '54/'56

stedelijk van abbemuseum eindhoven

10 november tot 10 december 1956

dagelijks geopend van 10-17 uur

zondag van 13-17 uur

dinsdag en donderdagavond van 20-22 uur

stedelijk museum
amsterdam

Hedendaagse kunst
Plakat
95×64 cm
Stedelijk Museum Amsterdam, 1971

(Left)
Art Director/Designer: Wim Crouwel
Year: 1956

(Right)
Art Director/Designer: Wim Crouwel
Year: 1971

INTERNATIONALE
ECONOMISCH-HISTORISCHE
TENTOONSTELLING

4 JULI
15 SEPT.
1929

SCHILDERIJEN
MINIATUREN
GOBELINS
DOCUMENTEN
MODELLEN
GRAFIEK ENZ

STEDELIJK MUSEUM
AMSTERDAM

Art Director/Designer: Hendriurs T. Wijdeveld
Year: ca. 1929

A SHEET OF PAPER

Rémy Zaugg

Art Director/Designer: Walter Nikkels
Year: 1987

(Left)
Art Director/Designer: Pieter Brattinga
Year: 1984
(c)1998 Artists Rights Society (ARS), New York/Beeldrecht, Amsterdam

(Right)
Art Director/Designer: Walter Nikkels
Year: 1989

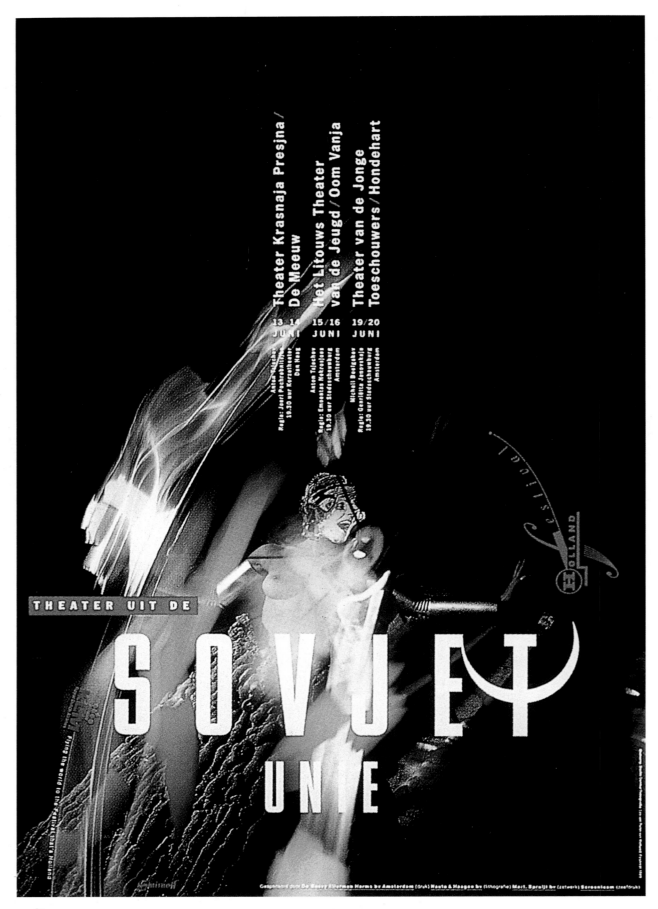

Art Director/Designer: Studio Dumbar
Photographer: Lex van Pieterson
Client: Holland Festival
Year: 1987

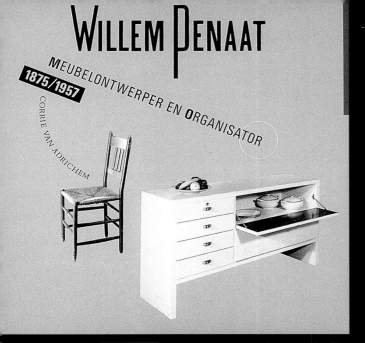

WILLEM PENAAT

1875/1957

MEUBELONTWERPER EN ORGANISATOR

CORRIE VAN ADRICHEM

MICHEL de KLERK

FRANS VAN BURKOM

1884/1923

BOUW- EN MEUBELKUNSTENAAR

Jan Buijs

CHRIS REHORST

INTERIEURS

1889/1961

Frits Spanjaard

MARG VAN DER BURGH

BINNENHUISARCHITECT

1889/1978

Art Director/Designer: Vorm Vijf

typografie is de ordening van tekst op papier

Typografie is de ordening van tekst op papier. Deze ordening kan er bij eenzelfde tekst heel verschillend uitzien omdat de mogelijkheden binnen de typografie van drukwerk zo gevarieerd zijn. De diversiteit bij

Typografie van drukwerk

verschillende soorten teksten is nog groter. De ordening van tekst op een formulier is nu eenmaal een andere dan die in een jaarverslag, zoals de ordening van tekst in een literatuurlijst er weer anders zal uitzien dan die van een promotiefolder. Voor de huisstijl van het Ministerie van Onderwijs en Wetenschappen zijn een aantal typografische richtlijnen ontwikkeld die in hun toepassing ervoor zorgen dat een bepaalde typografische kwaliteit gewaarborgd is en die ervoor

zorgen dat het drukwerk van het ministerie herkenbaar is. Heel kenmerkend zijn de horizontaal verspringende tekstblokken, zoals toegepast in deze brochure. De typografische richtlijnen kunnen een zeer dynamische, contrastrijke of gevarieerde typografie mogelijk maken, maar evengoed een ingetogen of bescheiden typografie. De richtlijnen zijn duidelijk en gedetailleerd, in veel gevallen zelfs erg strikt. Ze kunnen zelfs zó strikt zijn dat nauwkeurig omschreven wordt hoe aanhalingstekens gezet moeten en hoe opsommingen in de tekst genummerd dienen te zijn. Maar waar het gaat om de ordening van de tekst wordt weer veel ruimte gelaten aan de individuele ontwerper. Het is dan ook niet zo dat in de typografie geen plaats voor creativiteit zou zijn.

Het is dan ook niet zo dat in de typografie geen plaats voor creativiteit zou zijn

Art Director/Designer: Frans Lienshout

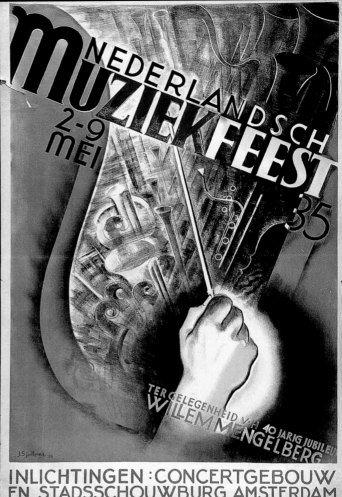

(Left)
Designer: Unknown
Year: ca. 1930
Client: Muziekschool Toonkunst, Utrecht, The Netherlands
Printer: Linoleumdruk J. Van Boekhoven

(Right)
Designer: J. Sjollema
Year: 1935
Printer: L. van Leer & Co. N.V. Amsterdam

HOLLANDSCHE SCHOUWBURG
DIRECTEUR = LOUIS · DE · VRIES

DE ROODE DANSERES

VAN CHARLES HENRI · HIRSCH
REGIE: LOUIS · DE · VRIES · DECORS = JAAP · VAN · DAM

Designer: Willy Gluiter
Year: 1914

REIST PER

SPOOR

VEILIG
SNEL
COMFORTABEL

OFFSETDRUK SMEETS WEERT.

Design: v.d.V
Year: 1932
Printer: Smeets Weert

Designer: Antoon Kurvers
Year: 1926

Designer: Antoon Kurvers
Year: 1926
Printer: Drukkerij van Leer Amsterdam

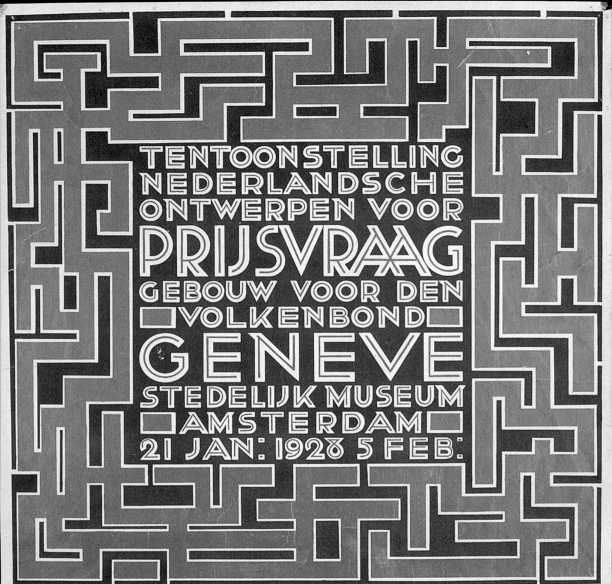

TENTOONSTELLING NEDERLANDSCHE ONTWERPEN VOOR PRIJSVRAAG GEBOUW VOOR DEN VOLKENBOND GENEVE STEDELIJK MUSEUM AMSTERDAM 21 JAN: 1928 5 FEB:

NEODRUK AHREND

H.Th. WIJDEVELD

Designer: Hendriurs T. Wijdeveld
Year: 1928
Client: Stedelijk Museum, Amsterdam

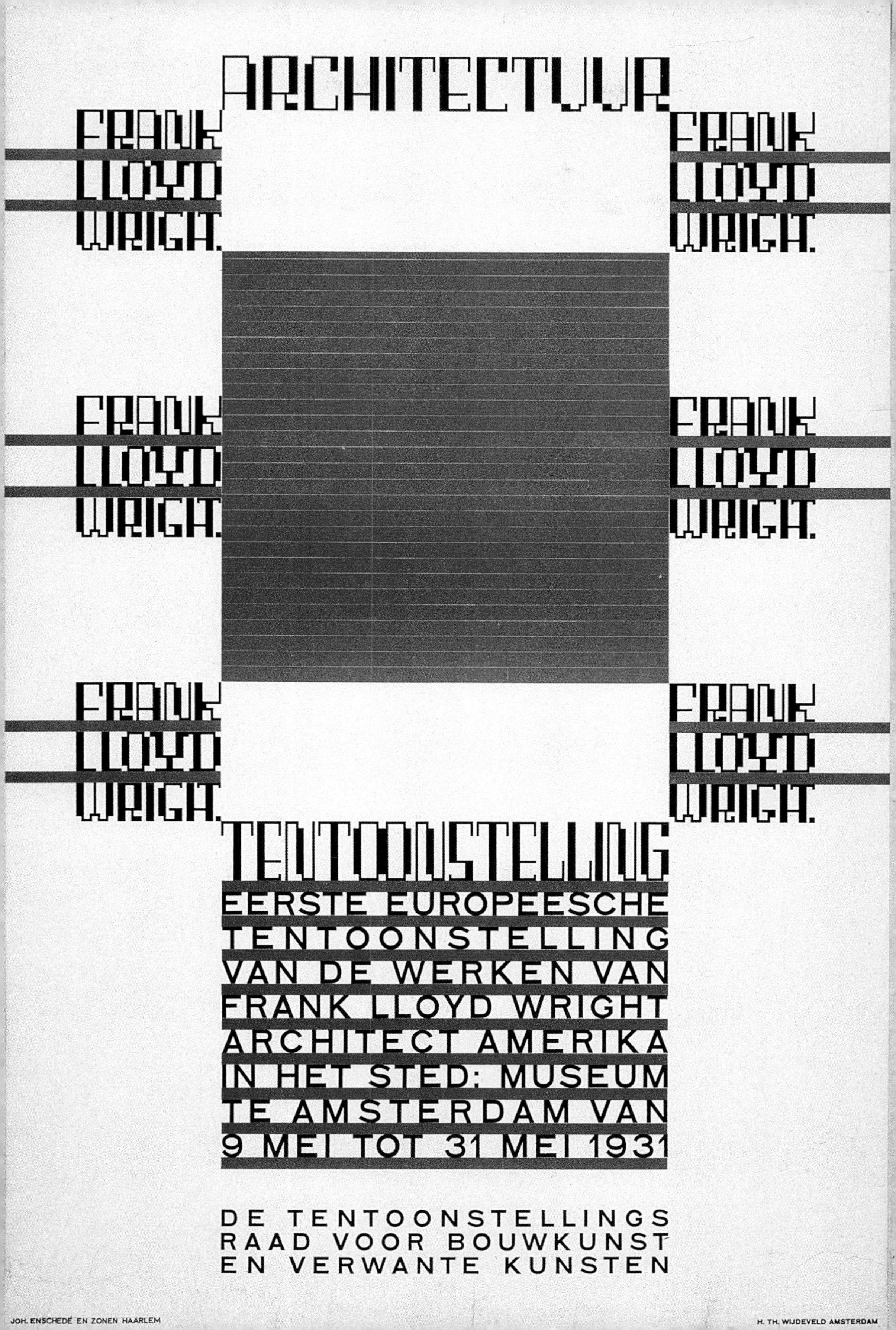

ARCHITECTUUR

FRANK LLOYD WRIGHT.

FRANK LLOYD WRIGHT.

FRANK LLOYD WRIGHT.

FRANK LLOYD WRIGHT.

FRANK LLOYD WRIGHT.

FRANK LLOYD WRIGHT.

TENTOONSTELLING

EERSTE EUROPEESCHE
TENTOONSTELLING
VAN DE WERKEN VAN
FRANK LLOYD WRIGHT
ARCHITECT AMERIKA
IN HET STED: MUSEUM
TE AMSTERDAM VAN
9 MEI TOT 31 MEI 1931

DE TENTOONSTELLINGS
RAAD VOOR BOUWKUNST
EN VERWANTE KUNSTEN

JOH. ENSCHEDÉ EN ZONEN HAARLEM   H. TH. WIJDEVELD AMSTERDAM

Designer: Unknown
Year: 1928

Designer: Unknown
Client: F. Addegon en Co., Amsterdam
Printer: F. Addegon en Co., Amsterdam

VEILIG DOOR VOORZORG

NILLMIJ

LEVENSVERZEKERING MIJ.

DELFTSCHE SLAOLIE

N O F

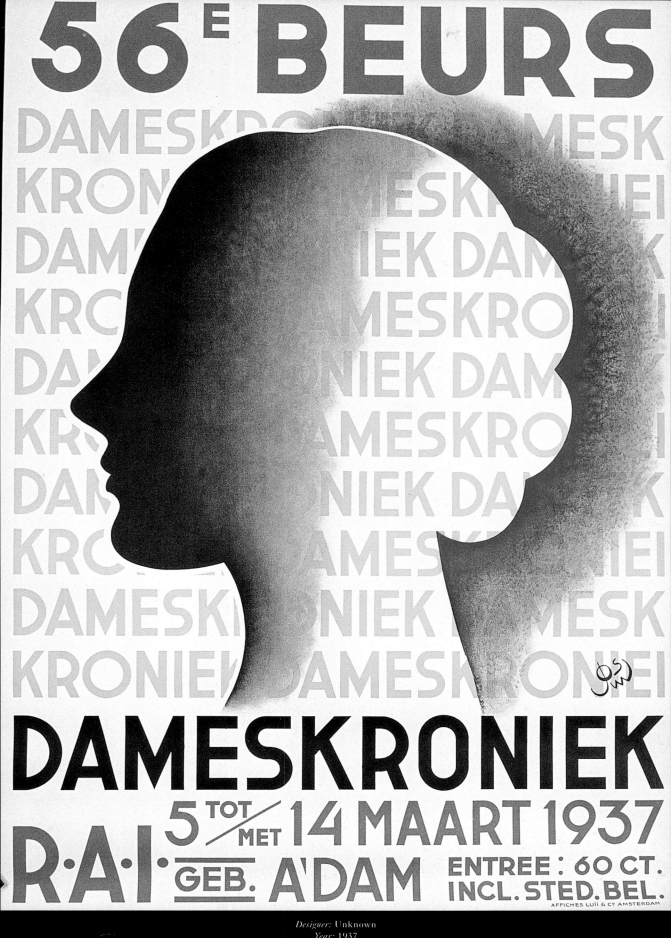

Designer: Unknown
Year: 1937
Printer: Affiches Luii & Co. Amsterdam

Designer: Jacob Jangma
Year: 1932
Printer: Offsetdruck A.v.d. Weerd, Arnhem

IN HET
ROODE
GEZIN
● DE
NIEUWE
ROODE
KRANT

VOLKSBLAD

VOOR · FRIESLAND

● 20
CENT
● PER
WEEK

HET · GELD · DUBBEL · WAARD

JAN ROT

Designer: Jan Rot
Client: Volksblad voor Friesland

Designer: Adriaan Joh. van't Hoff
Year: 1925
Client: Holland-Amerika Linie
Printer: Lankhout, Haag, Holland

Designer: Machiel Wilmink
Year: 1927
Client: Rotterdamsche Lloyd
Printer: Ned. Rotogravure, Leiden

MART STAM

DE ARCHITEKT

Designer: Paul Schuitema
Year: 1972

Designer: Unknown
Year: 1958
Client: Centraal Museum Utrecht
Printer: Steendruckerij de Jong & Co., Hilversum

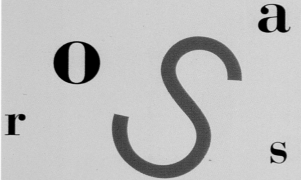

Designer: Pieter Roozen
Year: 1993
Client: Holland Festival, Amsterdam

het nieuwe bouwen

in

rotterdam

1920-1960

boymans-van beuningen

dinsdag t/m zaterdag van 10 tot 17 uur
zon- en feestdagen 11 tot 17 uur
maandagen en 1 januari gesloten

28 november 1982 t/m 6 februari 1983

Designer: Wim Crouwel
Year: 1983
Printer: De Jong & Co.

Vrijdag 8 augustus Zaterdag 9 augustus Zondag 10 augustus

Vrijdag 8 augustus	Zaterdag 9 augustus	Zondag 10 augustus
JUST FRIENDS	FREE FAIR + 8	HET WATERLAND KWINTET
ARTHUR BLYTHE PLUS HAMIET BLUIETT	JACK WILKINS TRIO & RED RODNEY & IRA SULLIVAN	GERRY MULLIGAN AND HIS CONCERT ORCHESTRA
MEETING NINE	HERBIE WHITE KWINTET	TEDDY EDWARDS QUARTET
JIMMY WITHERSPOON & THE EARLE WARREN QUINTET	RED HOLLOWAY QUARTET & GEORGE "BIG NICK" NICHOLAS	MR. SLIM'S WONDERLAND STEELBAND

INTERNATIONAAL

JazzFestival

8 9 10 AUG 80

AMSTERDAM

DE MEERVAART

GEORGANISEERD
door de Nos in samenwerking met de Brt,
het Molde International Jazz Festival, de Vara, Wagons-Lits en De Meervaart.

TIJDEN
tussen 20.30 en ± 03.00 uur: Concerten
's middags vanaf 12.00 uur: Podium, Workshops o.l.v. Teddy Edwards en Theo Loevendie

ONTWERP: FRANS LASÉS / DRUK: VAN BARNEVELD

Designer: Joost Swarte
Year: 1983
Client: Parc Marignac, Lancy, Genève

Kieler Woche

22.-30. Juni 1991

Design: Ben Bos
Design Firm: Total Design
Year: 1991
Client: Kieler Woche Büro, Kiel

Designers: Bob van Dijk, Gert Dumbar, Lex van Pieterson
Year: 1993
Client: Theater Zeebelt, Den Haag
Printer: Affiche Européenne, Omnimark

Graduation'93

Expositie 49 jonge industriële vormgevers afgestudeerd in november 1992 en mei 1993 aan de Akademie Industriële Vormgeving Eindhoven

Exhibition of 49 young industrial designers graduated in November 1992 and May 1993 at the Akademie Industriële Vormgeving Eindhoven

Beurs van Berlage

Damrak, Amsterdam
ingang Beursplein
dagelijks 11 - 17 uur
vrijdag 11 - 22 uur
Entree gratis, catalogus verkrijgbaar

Damrak, Amsterdam
entrance Beursplein
daily 11 am - 5 pm
Friday 11 am - 10 pm
Free entry, catalogue available

Industriële Vormgeving

21-24 oktober 1993

Designer: Guus Ros
Year: 1993

SONSBEEK 93
INTERNATIONAL ART EXHIBITION

5·6·93 – 26·9·93
SEVEN DAYS A WEEK 10.00 – 17.00

ARNHEM NL
VISITORSGUIDE/TICKETS: VILLA PARK SONSBEEK AND GEMEENTE
MUSEUM ARNHEM/HOLLAND INFORMATION 85·429044 PGEM from VSB FONDS

Designer: Unknown
Year: 1993
Client: Sonsbeek International Art Exhibition

Exchange 2

Shedhalle Zürich

1993

Exhibition June 18 to July 25

Artists and Theoreticians in Residence June 15 to 25

Lectures: June 18, 19, 20, 21 - 18.00 and 19.30 hours

Organization of Lectures in co-operation with Schule und Museum für Gestaltung, Zürich, Interventionen

Shedhalle, Rote Fabrik, Seestrasse 395, CH-8038 Zürich, Tel.: 01-481 59 50, Fax: 01-482 92 10

Opening hours: Tuesday through Friday 14 to 20 hours / Saturday and Sunday 14 to 17 hours

e Keep
Juni, 21 Uhr

edhalle
e Fabrik, Seestrasse 395
ich, Tel. 01-481 59 50

Designer: Den Haag Ontwerpwerk
Year: 1993
Client: Stadt Frankfurt am Main
Printer: Drukkerij Dombosch Raamsdonksveer

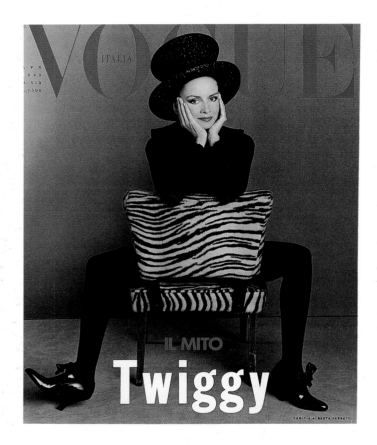

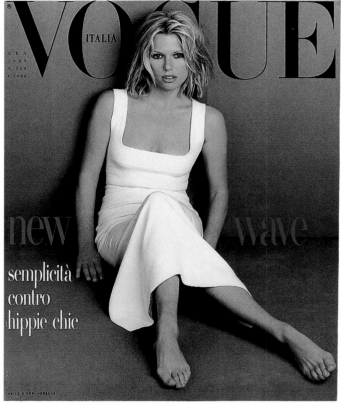

Art Director: Luca Stoppini
Photographer: Steven Meisel
Fashion Editor: Joe McKenna (left), Lori Goldstein (right)
Publisher: Edizione Condé Nast (Vogue Italia)

Q

fall's refined appeal

uiet luxury, considered line, beautiful fabrics: These are the qualities that epitomize the new elegance that underlies fall's flashier changes. These are clothes beyond the seasonal vagaries of fashion, yet within their timeless appeal show real, substantive changes that are absolutely of the moment. A sweeping black evening dress that bares only the shoulders in a statement of subtle exposure. A soft gray coatdress worn with matching trousers, in a completely original variation on the suit. "Elegance is understatement," says Calvin Klein. "The woman should stand out; the clothes should not overtake her." There's an integrity of design that allows these pieces to stand on their own: They don't need the glittery camouflage of a wristful of bracelets or strands of necklaces to look finished. "That ethic of jeweled, fussy, scalloped, and teased is just not in my world anymore," says Isaac Mizrahi. "Now a scent, a defined eyebrow, is all you need." Impeccable in balance, cut, and proportion, these are the clothes that, by virtue of their practicality, their lack of pretension, are the foundation of a great wardrobe. A new grace comes to evening. Opposite page: Black viscose/Lycra turtleneck, drop-waist dress, about $1375, by Donna Karan.

AdD

Alex Liberman e Erwin Blumenteld (Vogue)/
Leagas Delaney/ Agência: Talent/ ADC Show/
Anúncio Brasileiros/
Jean Paul Goude, etc.

tor: Oswaldo Miranda *Designer:* Alex Liberman *Photographer:* Erwin Blumenfeld *Publication:* AdD *Publisher:* Casa de Ideías Editora

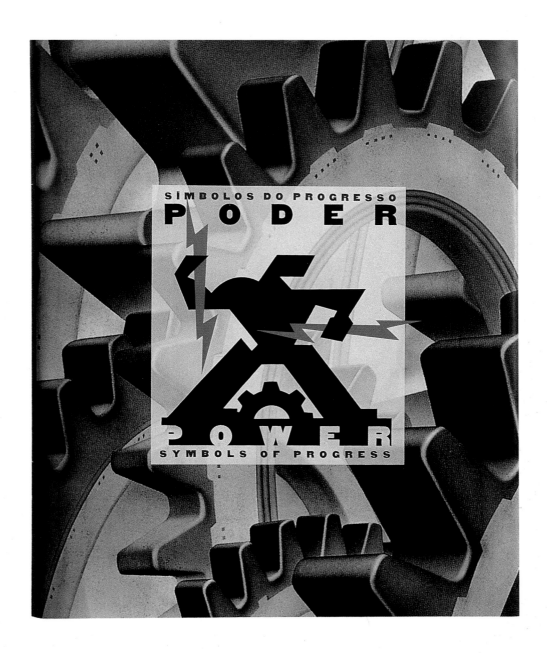

Art Director/Designer: Oswaldo Miranda
Publisher: Casa de Ideías Editora (In-house)

LOSE

"to ensure our Belgian chocolates

none of their smoothness, we strictly

CONTROL

their temperature and humidity."

Häagen-Dazs

Dedicated to Pleasure.

"I ALWAYS SAY

THAT HÄAGEN-DAZS IS THE

delicate

COMBINATION OF THE

WORLD'S FINEST INGREDIENTS

WITH JUST A

touch

OF INSPIRATION."

KEN SNIDER, DEVELOPMENT DIRECTOR.

Häagen-Dazs

Dedicated to pleasure.

"Artificial flavours and colours have no part to

PLAY

in the Häagen-Dazs story. Consequently we spend much of our

TIME

searching for the finest ingredients".

Häagen-Dazs

DEDICATED TO PLEASURE

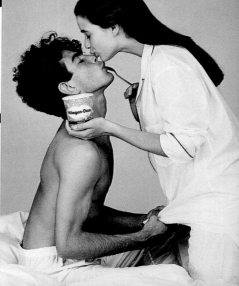

Director: Rooney Carruthers *Photographer:* Barry Lategan (top), Jeanloup Sieff (middle, bottom) *Copywriter:* Larry Barker
Agency: Bartle Bogle Hegarty *Client:* Häagen-Dazs

TOO BAD FAMILIES TORN APART BY SUBSTANCE ABUSE AREN'T THIS EASY TO PUT BACK TOGETHER.

If you or someone you know is affected by alcohol or drug problems, call for help. 1-800-622-7422, 24 hours. Rhode Island Council On Alcoholism and Other Drug Dependence

Art Director: Greg Bokor
Copywriter: Kara Goodrich
Agency: Leonard Monahan Lubars & Kelly
Client: Rhode Island Council on Alcoholism & Other
Drug Dependence

Art Director/Designer/Copywriter: Louise Fili
Photographer: Ed Spiro
Design Firm: Louis Fili Ltd.
Client: Cincinnati Art Directors Club
Paper: Potlatch Millcraft
Typeface: Futura Book, Excelsior Script
Printer: Pepper Printing
Announcement of speaking engagement at the Art
Directors Club of Cincinnati.

Art Director: KYM Abrams
Designer: Mike Stees
Agency: KYM Abrams Design
Client: Illinois Film Office
Guide promoting film locations in Illinois.

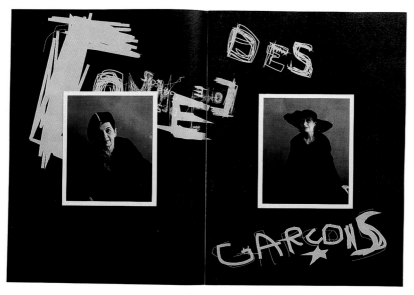

Art Director: Joerg Bauer *Designer:* Joerg Bauer *Illustrator:* Joerg Bauer *Photographer:* Ralf Schmerberg *Agency:* Jubel + Trubel *Client:* Horst Wanschura

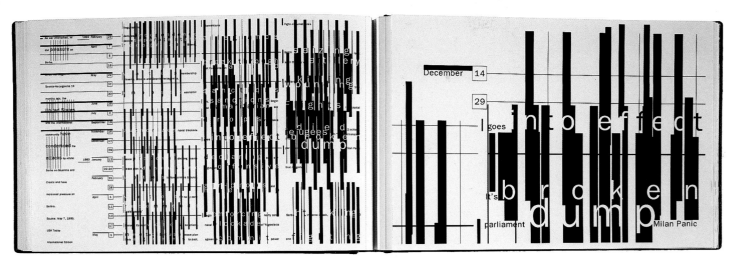

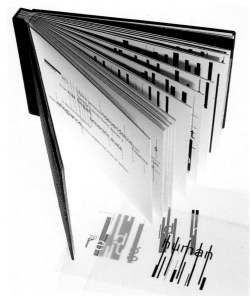

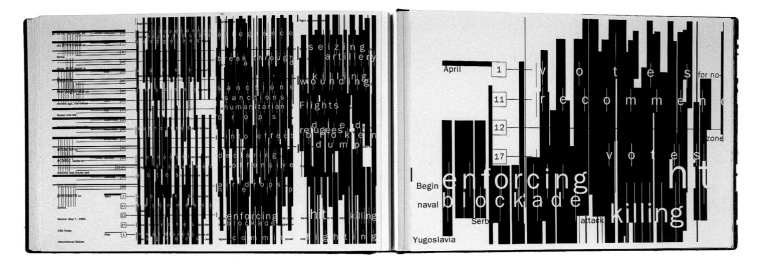

Art Director: Stéphanie Bolliger *Designer:* Stéphanie Bolliger *Client:* Stéphanie Bolliger *Design Firm:* Bolliger Design Studio

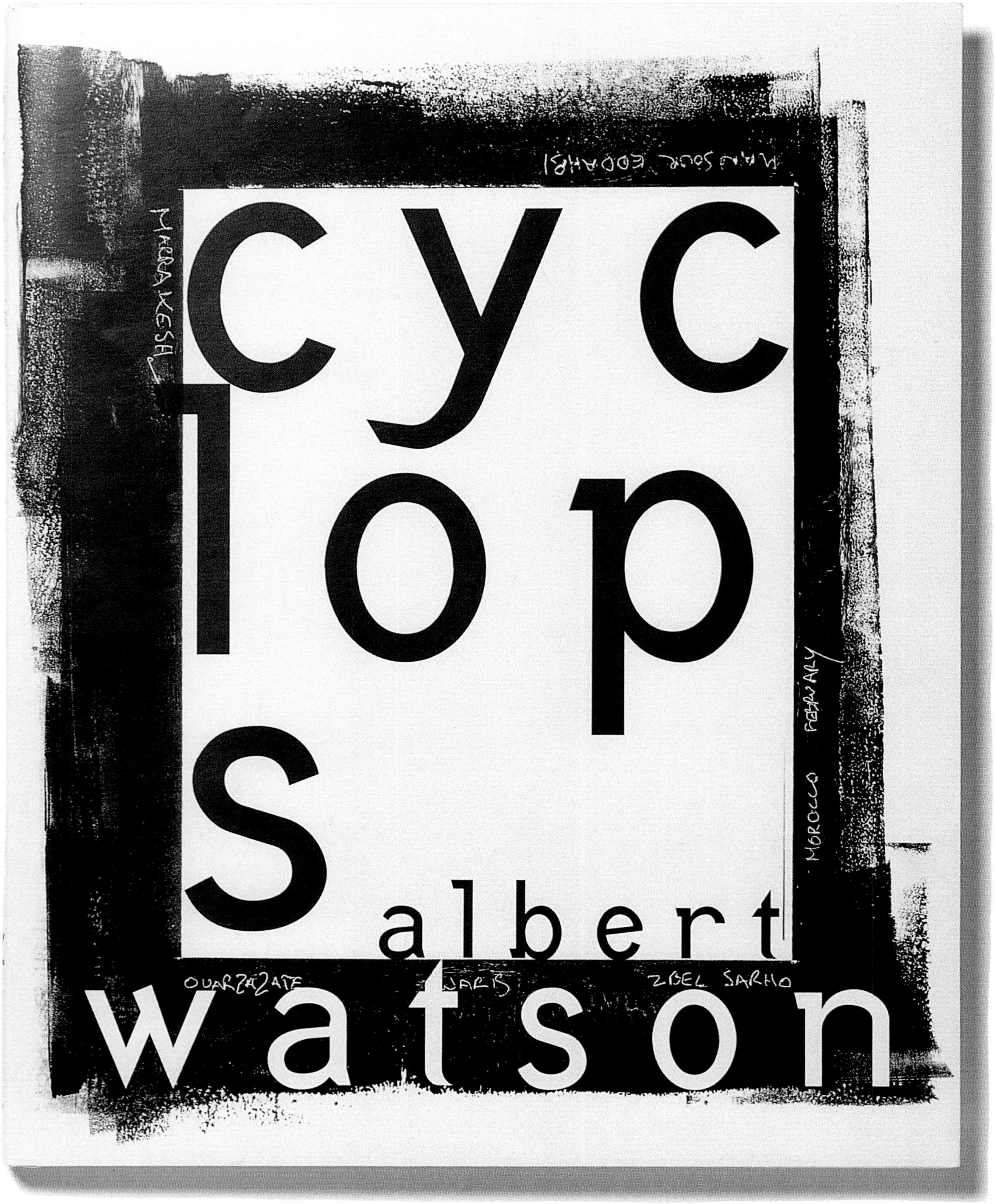
cyclops
albert
watson
MARRAKESH
MOROCCO FEBRUARY

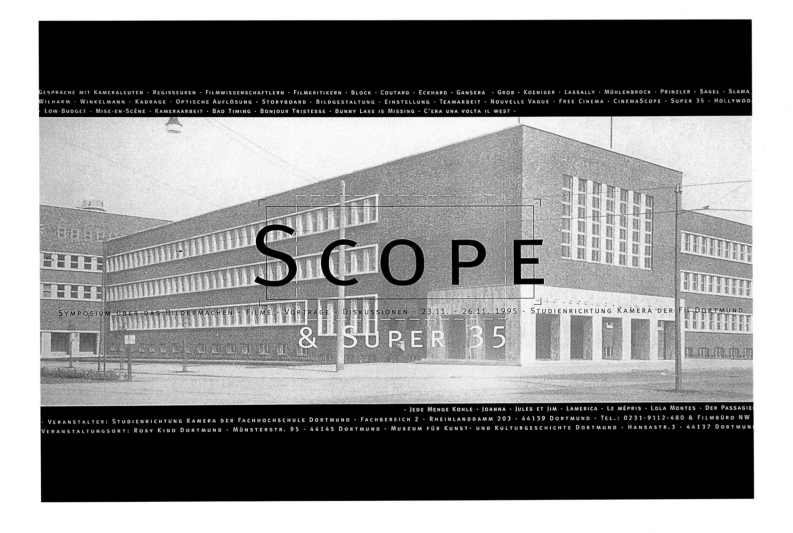

(Opposite)
Art Director/Designer: David Carson
Photographer: Albert Watson
Photo Editor: Laurie Kratochvil
Publisher: Callaway Editions

(This page)
Art Directors: Hans-Heinrich Sures, Ingo Eulen
Designer: Hans-Heinrich Sures
Client: Fachhochschule Dortmund
Typeface: Meta Caps
Printer: COD Color-Offset-Druck

(This page) *Art Director:* Fred Woodward *Publisher:* Little Brown *Typeface:* Goudy Italian *Paper:* NPI Matte Art *Printer:* Dai Nippon
(Opposite) *Designer:* Pierre Mendell *Photographer:* Hans Hansen *Copywriter:* Vitra *Client:* Vitra *Agency:* Mendell & Oberer

Central Park, designed by Fredrick Law Olmsted and Calvert Vaux, is a masterpiece of 19th Century landscape architecture, and the most frequently used urban park in the United States. The Central Park Conservancy is dedicated to the care and upkeep of this treasured landmark, providing a permanent endowment for landscape maintenance as well as funding educational, recreational and volunteer programs for the Park's current and future visitors.

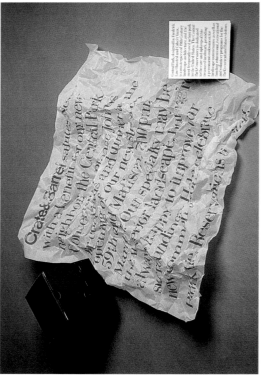

Art Director: Alessandro Franchini
Agency: Crate and Barrel (in-house)
Graphic program introducing first Crate &
Barrel store to the New York City market.

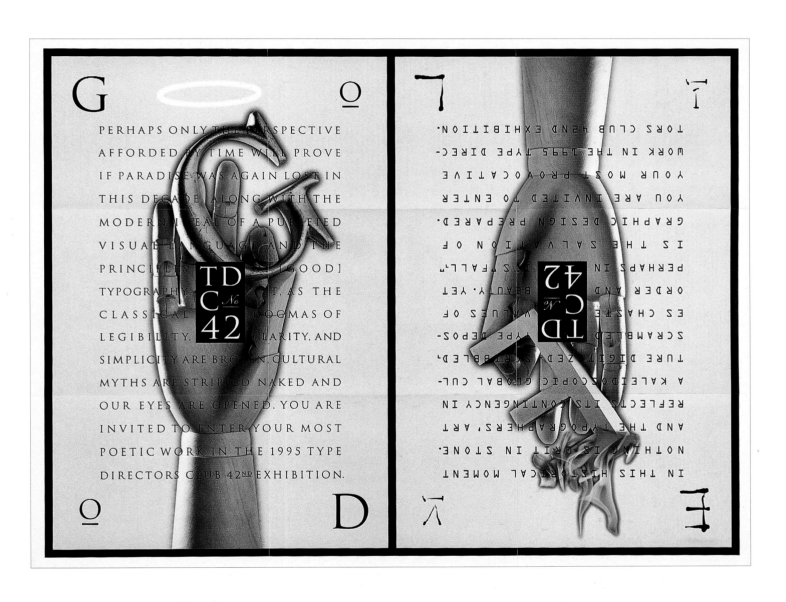

Left panel:

G O

PERHAPS ONLY THE PERSPECTIVE AFFORDED BY TIME WILL PROVE IF PARADISE WAS AGAIN LOST IN THIS DECADE, ALONG WITH THE MODERN IDEAL OF A PURIFIED VISUAL LANGUAGE AND THE PRINCIPLES OF [GOOD] TYPOGRAPHY. PERHAPS NOT, AS THE CLASSICAL DOGMAS OF LEGIBILITY, CLARITY, AND SIMPLICITY ARE BROKEN, CULTURAL MYTHS ARE STRIPPED NAKED AND OUR EYES ARE OPENED. YOU ARE INVITED TO ENTER YOUR MOST POETIC WORK IN THE 1995 TYPE DIRECTORS CLUB 42ND EXHIBITION.

O D

TDC No 42

Right panel:

IN THIS HISTORICAL MOMENT NOTHING IS WRIT IN STONE. AND THE TYPOGRAPHERS' ART REFLECTS ITS CONTINGENCY IN A KALEIDOSCOPIC GLOBAL CULTURE DIGITIZED (SCRAMBLED), TYPE DEPOSES CHASTE VALUES OF ORDER AND BEAUTY. YET PERHAPS IN ITS PRATFALL IS THE SALVATION OF GRAPHIC DESIGN PREPARED. YOU ARE INVITED TO ENTER YOUR MOST PROVOCATIVE WORK IN THE 1995 TYPE DIRECTORS CLUB 42ND EXHIBITION.

TDC No 42

Art Director/Designer: Michael Vanderbyl *Agency:* Vanderbyl Design *Photographer:* Gaby Brink *Client:* Type Directors Club *Printer:* Quality House of Graphics, Inc.
Competition announcement discussing good and bad typography.

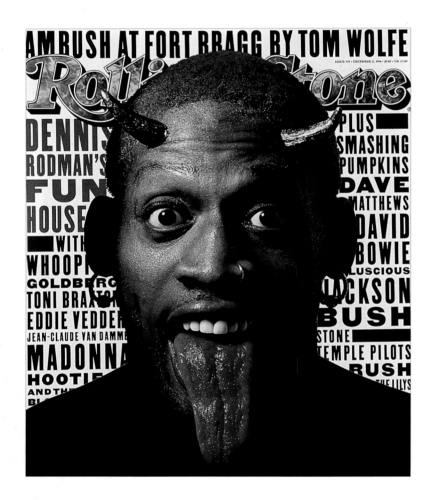

Art Director: Fred Woodward
Designer: Fred Woodward
Photographer: Albert Watson
Photo Editor: Jodi Peckman

Publisher: Wenner Media
Art Director: Fred Woodward
Designer: Gail Anderson
Photographer: Albert Watson

8 1

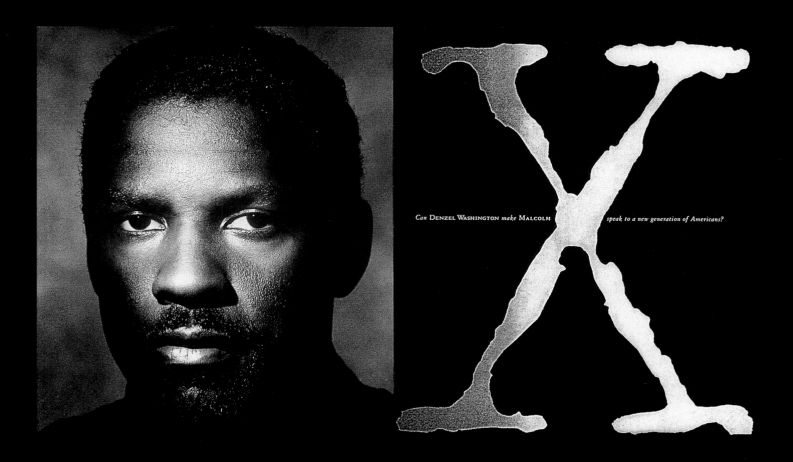

Can DENZEL WASHINGTON *make* MALCOLM speak to a new generation of Americans?

Publisher: Wenner Media
Art Director: Fred Woodward
Designer: Gail Anderson
Photographer: Albert Watson

(Opposite)
Art Director: Dan Olson
Designers: Dan Olson, Todd Bartz, Eden Fahlen
Photographer: Lev Tushavs
Agency: Duffy Design
Client: Flagstone Brewery

(This page)
Art Director: Ken-Ya Hara
Designer: Ken-Ya Hara
Agency: Nippon Design Center, Inc.
Client: The Nikka Whisky Distilling Co., Ltd.

(This page)
Art Director: Alan Chan
Designers: Alan Chan, Peter Lo
Agency: Alan Chan Design Company
Client: Davinci Co. Ltd, Kosta Boda

(Opposite)
Art Director/Designer: Steve Sandstrom
Agency: Sandstrom Design
Client: Tazo Tea Company
Typeface: Nickolas Cochin, Nuptial, Garamond No. 3

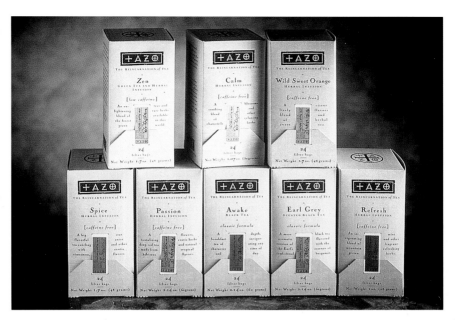

(This page) *Designer:* Henrik Barends *Publisher:* In de Knipscheer ■ Cover art from one book in a series containing poems by young authors.
(Opposite) *Art Director:* Paula Scher *Designers:* Paula Scher, Ron Louie, Lisa Mazur *Design Firm:* Pentagram Design *Client:* The Public Theater

Art Director: Kurt Koepfle
Designers: Paula Scher, Ron Louie, Lisa Mazur
Design Firm: Pentagram Design
Client: Public Theater

For this edition of *Graphis Typography*, we invited prominent designers to create their own spreads featuring their favorite typographic designs from the past three years. They were asked to explain their choices and, if they wished, to comment on type trends today. Designers were also encouraged to choose a piece by someone whom they admire and to comment on it. Finally, they were asked to name their five favorite typefaces. • The results of these efforts are reproduced in the following spreads. We have done our best not to interfere with their choices and have added only grammatical corrections where it was necessary. • In some instances, designers provided remarks or captions and selected favorite typefaces, but did not include them in their spreads. This information can be found in the Designers' Remarks on pages 210-211.

The following is an excerpt from a high school graduation speech given by Spenser Somers, who died in 1990 at age 18 from cancer.

I guess I used to think that life is like a long highway. I was just cruising along on what I thought at the time to be an endless road. I, however, got stuck with a faulty engine, and it forced me to stop cruising and to pull over onto the shoulder and to start walking. And it was once I started walking that I began to see all the beauty that was only a colorful blur before. And once I began to walk, the wind didn't blow through my hair, 'cause I didn't have any, and instead of music there were the songs of the birds and the crickets to be heard. But once I started to walk and once I took off my shades I began to see things clearly for the first time. I began to see that success should not be measured by grades or dollar signs, but by how often you laugh and by how many people you can make smile in a day. I began to see that once you are at peace with God, peace with your fellow man comes as well as peace with yourself. And I began to see that our earthly highway not only has plenty of detours and potholes, but it isn't nearly as long as I once thought.

This piece was designed for the New York Times as a commentary on the New Year for the January 1st edition. As I pulled together all the various scraps of type I had saved during the year, I came across a graduation speech written by a boy who was dying of cancer. It seemed to put the idea of a single year into perspective, bringing home our own mortality and how little time we actually have left. I chose this piece because my use of typography is based not only on how the type looks, but what the words actually say.

My typographic aesthetic is based on printed scraps of paper, labels, packages, ticket stubs, dry cleaner receipts, deli numbers and other vernacular sources.

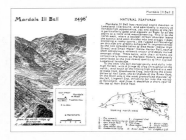

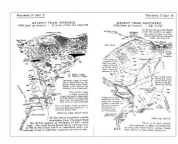

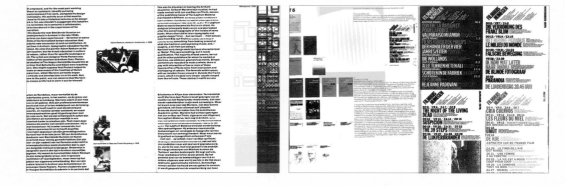

My ideas have always come more from things read, from discussions with design friends and teaching colleagues than from things seen. I wrote once "I have no heroes: only the stone-cutters and the silent scribes," but I was lying. The books reproduced on the left are important to me mainly because of the unity of thought and expression they portray.

A Wainwright | *A pictorial guide to the Lakeland Fells, being an illustrated account of a study and exploration of the mountains in the English Lake District* | Westmorland Gazette, Kendal, seven books between 1955 and 1966 | Book two shown, *The far eastern fells* | 1958 | 312pp Hb | full of maps and illus.

These books and Wainwright's own models, the maps of the Ordnance Survey and *An inventory of the historical monuments in Westmorland* (Royal Commission on Historical Monuments, 1936) were the books I grew up with.

Entirely handwritten, they combine notes, routes to the summits, personal recollections, history, anecdote and detailed maps. They are models of good information design right down to the format—small enough to take walking—and have not been equalled in the field of guide book design.

The four Gospels | Golden Cockerel Press | 1931 | originally 276pp Hb | approx. 8 full-page, 32 substantial and 14 minor illus. | reproduced from 1988 reprint (includes extra 16pp section of notes) September Press, Wellingborough.

This is very much the product of Eric Gill's vision and includes his typeface (Golden Cockerel), the ranged-left setting, and his incredible woodcuts. Not one is a pure illustration; all involve letters. A perfect marriage of form and content, of text and image.

Karel Martens | *Printed matter\drukwerk* | Hyphen Press 1996 | 144pp chinese binding, flapped and french-folded Pb jacket | many illus.

The work and thoughts of this important Dutch designer given sensitive and intriguing graphic form. Prelims and end-matter printed black only, the work reproduced—a mixture of actual size and dramatic reductions—in full colour with matter-of-fact commentary printed in cyan.

Much of my early work was concerned with making a strong visual impact: typography for looking at first and foremost. This approach is fine for display uses but the kind of work I've been concerned with over the past two years has been predominately catalogue and bookwork. In certain cases my approach can be seen as an exploration of ways to articulate the paragraph within the constraints of readability.

I used to say I worked on my own, but with this kind of work I am very aware that this is no longer the case, the work shown opposite represents fruitful collaborations with editors, authors, publishers, fellow designers and the occasional assistant.

Gerlinde Gabriel (Ed.) | Exhibition guides for series *Conceptual Art in Germany since 1968*: *Reiner Ruthenbeck* (1994, 24pp + 4pp Pb cover, 8 illus.) *Imi Knoebel* (1995, 20pp + 4pp Pb cover, 8 illus.) *Anna & Bernhard Blume* (1995, 20pp + 4pp Pb cover, 7 illus.) *Felix Droese* (1996, 20pp + 4pp Pb cover, 8 illus.) | Goethe Institut London

A series design whose common links are size, the use of a large solid of colour on the cover and 5mm leading for the text. The spread shown—for the essay 'Imprecisions of a precise artist: ten key words for Reiner Ruthenbeck' by Bernhard Holeczek—uses indents dictated by the length of the 'key' word.

John Maizels | *Raw Creation* | Phaidon 1996 | 240pp Hb | 420 illus.

The idea for the design came from the text itself—direct and enthusiastic, not a linear philosophical discourse. The text column width is a constant 99mm ensuring easy reading, but paragraphs are aligned from the point where the previous one ends. Such staggering of the text allows pictures to be placed closely to relevant passages of text. Footnotes are always at hand and turned sideways in the marginal column. Quotations by the artists appear in a larger point size and run the full width of the text area.

Directory 97/98 | Central Saint Martins College of Art & Design 1996 | 64pp + 2pp throw-out + 6pp Pb cover | 80 illus.

Designed with Ian Hands. All the typefaces used (other than the college name in compulsory Baskerville on the cover) were designed by ex-students or staff. The cover shows the grid and avoids the problem of finding an image to sum up the college. The information pages make the most of exaggerated paragraph indents and 'internal vertical justification' to articulate the text.

Christmas card 1996

Text arranged according to the structure of the sentence and a response to John Tavener's setting of *God is with us* (vc 5 45035 2).

David Jury (Ed.) | *Typographic 49* | STD 1996 | 20pp + 4pp Pb cover | 23 illus.

Extent and format were given at start, too much space! Grid is three-and-a-half columns arranged asymmetrically, position of half-column (for footnotes and captions) alternates from one article to the next. Every paragraph occupies one column, articles overlap emphasising continuity of theme within the issue.

Adam Lowe (Ed.) | *Digital prints* | Permaprint 1997 | 64pp Hb | 7 illus.

Text areas based loosely traditional models with generous margins. Each essay uses a different typeface to reflect its theme. Essay shown—'Indiscrete affairs' by Brian Smith—set in Beowolf. Footnotes occupy as many of four narrower columns as is necessary, always appear on the relevant page and introduce an element of asymmetry.

All work reproduced 20% actual size.

Reiner Ruthenbeck

Imi Knoebel

Anna & Bernhard Blume

Felix Droese

John Maizels **RAW CREATION** Outsider Art and beyond

with an introduction by Roger Cardinal

PHAIDON

directory

Central Saint Martins 97 / 98
College of Art & Design
THE LONDON INSTITUTE

HOW TO APPLY

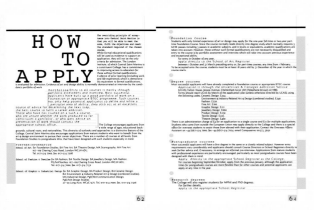

WONDERFUL COUNSELLOR!
THE MIGHTY GOD, THE EVERLASTING
FATHER, THE PRINCE OF PEACE.
CHRIST IS BORN!
CHRIST IS BORN! CHRIST IS BORN!

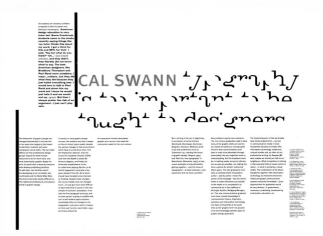

CAL SWANN typography is too important to be taught to designers

Jf it plese ony man spirituel or temporel to bye ony
pyes of two and thre comemoraciõs of salisburi vse
enpryntid after the forme of this preset lettre whiche
ben wel and truly correct, late hym come to westmo;
nester in to the almonesrye at the reed pale and he shal
haue them good chepe ∴∴

Supplico stet cedula

Caxton's advertisement c.1477. Actual size.
Courtesy of the Bodleian Library, Oxford
Unjustified, ranged left and centred all in one elegant layout.
The copy is also a model of clarity.

My greeting card to the late Paul Rand on his 80th birthday.
The inscription reads: 'to the evergreen Paul Rand.'

Birdsall, Derek Walter, RDI; freelance graphic designer;
b 1 Aug. 1934; *s* of Frederick Birdsall and Hilda Birdsall
(*née* Smith); *m* 1954, Shirley Thompson; three *s* one *d*.
Educ: King's Sch., Pontefract, Yorks; Wakefield Coll. of Art,
Yorks; Central Sch. of Arts and Crafts, London (NDD).
National Service, RAOC Printing Unit, Cyprus, 1955–57.
Lectr in Typographical Design, London Coll. of Printing,
1959–61; freelance graphic designer, working from his
studio in Covent Garden, later Islington, 1961–; Founding
Partner, Omnific Studios Partnership, 1983. Vis. Prof. of
Graphic Art and Design, Royal College of Art, 1987–88.
Consultant designer, The Independent Magazine, 1989–93;
Tutor and designer of the house-style for Prince of Wales's
Institute of Architecture, 1991; Design Consultant, National
Art Collections Fund, 1992–. has broadcast on TV and radio
on design subjects and his work; catalogue designs for major
museums throughout the world have won many awards, incl.
Gold Medal for 'Shaker Design', New York Art Directors'
Club, 1987. Mem., AGI. 1968–96, FCSD (FSIAD 1964);
RDI 1982; FRSA; Hon. FRCA 1988. *Publications*: (with C. H.
O'D. Alexander) Fischer v Spassky, 1972; (with C. H. O'D.
Alexander) A Book of Chess, 1974; (with Carlo M. Cippola)
The Technology of Man – a visual history, 1978; (with Bruce
Bernard) Lucian Freud, 1996. *Recreations*: chess, poker.
Address: 9 Compton Avenue, Islington, N1 2XD.
T: (0171) 359 1201. *Club*: Chelsea Arts.
Entry from *Who's Who*, 1997.

PPPPPPPP
PPPPPPPP
PPPPPPPP
PPPPPPPP
PPPPPPPP
PPPPPPPP
PPPPPPPP
PPPPPPPP
PPPPPPPP
PPPPPPPR

ABCDEFGHIJKLMNOPQR
STUVWXYZ
abcdefghijklmnopqrstuv
wxyz
1234567890

ABCDEFGHIJKLMNOPQRS
TUVWXYZ
abcdefghijklmnopqrstuv
wxyz
1234567890

The Singing Bird (officially named Luscinia svecica)
became one of my favorite pieces.
Desiging stamps is always a great challenge.
It is graphic design in miniature.
The regular size for stamps in Holland does not exceed the
dimensions of a 35mm slide.
Type is, of course, an important tool.
In this particular case it became more and more important
during the whole design process.
That is because the client kept adding information
that should be shown on the stamps.
To finance the Fepapost stamp exhibition,
customers had to pay an additional amount
(in this case an extra 70 cents).
I had to find a place for that.
The period of the exhibition was another unexpected addition
I had to position at a late stage of the development.

Reacting to a considerable number of "complicated"
recent Dutch stamp emissions, I wanted to design stamps
that were simple, straightforward and clear.
The typographic choices were, of course, part of "the game."
I hate typography on stamps
that can only be read with a magnifying-glass.
Stamps are public property.
The designer should not force people to use a magnifier.

I had discovered the charms of a new classic typeface,
Millbank, designed by the British typographer
Michael Harvey for the Tate Gallery, London.
I wanted to use this typeface for the postage value
and for the word Nederland on my series of stamps.
Through the Publications Department of the Tate,
I came into contact with Michael Harvey and got hold of
his Ellington series - the commercial version (Monotype) of
the Millbank typeface.

[Harvey loves jazz. So the name Ellington refers to
the Duke...]

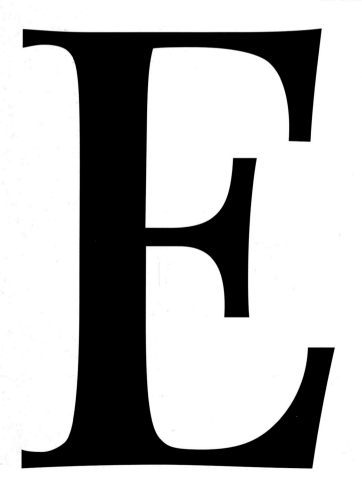

M+70

The open, very clear and linear character of Erik Spiekermann's
Meta normal allows for optimal legibility when it comes to
very small type. The small caps and the exceptional old style
numerals were another temptation to select Meta.
I decided that Ellington and Meta seemed a perfect match for
the text elements on my stamps.

Ben Bos AGI BNO
Amsterdam, the Netherlands

NEDERLAND

FEPAPOST 94
17 t/m 23 oktober

Luscinia
svecica

+70
80c

Blauwborst

+70
80c

NEDER

Commission:
Series of 3 stamps for the Dutch Post 1994

Subject:
FEPAPOST 94 International Stamp Exhibition
The Hague

DEN HAAG · 17 OKTOBER 1994
EERSTE DAG VAN UITGIFTE

On the Flaming Lips' *Drug Machine* 45 r.p.m. records sleeve, designer Art Chantry takes would-be limitations and amps them into typographic elegance.

Drug Machine maximizes the content of the pieces despite a budget which limited Chantry to the use of two colors. By overprinting two colors to make a third, Chantry creates a layered effect with a hierarchy of typographic elements.

Drug Machine is a design paradox, appearing alternately complex and simple. The koan-like quality of this piece comes not from mere virtuosity but from the choices the designer makes. The overlay of red on green to make a bent brown brushing over the cyclical white type of "Peace, Love, and Understanding" at once surprises and seems just so.

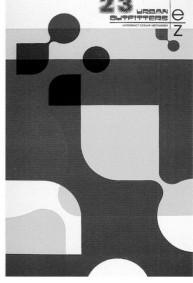

These three posters were designed as a series for the Urban Outfitters' 1996 fall campaign. Each poster intentionally emphasizes a certain design aspect: biologic *(lower right)*, geometric *(upper right)*, and typographic *(upper left)*.

Each individual poster was designed with the entire series and the printing process in mind. Continuity is maintained throughout the series by reconfiguring the Urban Outfitters' logo elements. Each poster was printed in an additional color configuration in which the cyan and magenta were switched (not shown), which changed the overall color cast.

Because it is a design based solely on a typographic solution, we feel the piece on the upper left was our best submission. Numbers are printed in yellow while the uppercase letters URBAN are cyan and magenta. We chose fonts that reminded us of our childhood and created the old-fashioned way – paste-up.

Art Director: Howard Brown
Designers: Howard Brown and Mike Calkins
Size: 24" x 38"
Colors: 3 color process
Paper: white uncoated cover stock

Città di Asiago. Assessorato all'Urbanistica. Piano Regolatore Generale di Asiago

Forum

Vittorio Gregotti, Augusto Cagnardi, Giorgio Cian, Paolo Costa

Giorgio Ferrari, Giorgio Franceschetti, Vittorio Iliceto, Mario Isnenghi

Ermanno Olmi, Mario Rigoni Stern. Conduce Sergio Frigo

Asiago : Orientare il futuro

Hotel Croce Bianca   **21.05.1994 Ore 18**

Opposite:
The poster is a trap.
The large color signs are the bait.
The text draws delicately balanced lines
which beg the eye to move.
But then it's already too late.
You have to read.

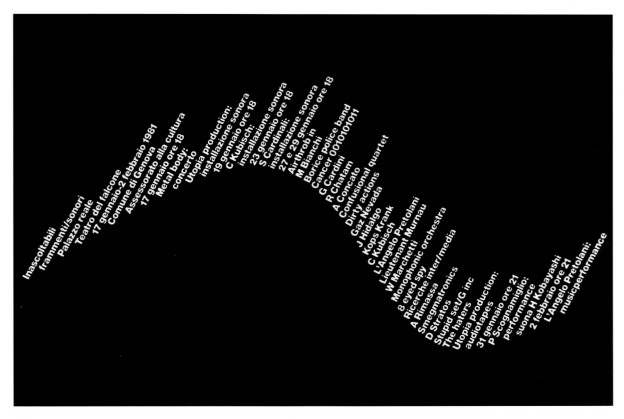

Above:
To AG Fronzoni. Against visual pollution.
The typographic performance is the message.
The message hits the mind rather than
the retina. And forces an effort
of interpretation.
A poster by Fronzoni does not wear out
with the message it conveys. It goes beyond.
It draws a path with the freedom
of visual poetry.

Favorite Typefaces: Bodoni, Gill Sans, Garamond, Futura, Caslon

At Estrus Records a new "logo" is created for every project undertaken, no matter how tiny or insignificant. Every poster or 45 rpm or full-blown CD has its own "identity." The net result is scores of fake "logos" designed by dozens of artists and designers—including Dave Crider, Frank Kozik, Coop, Alex Wald, Merinuk, etc., and even band members like Tim Kerr, Dave Holmes and The Makers. This obtuse activity has been going on for ten years. • Shown here is a sampling of the dozens of "logos" I personally concocted for the label. You'll notice a number of familiar images taken from various areas of cheezy pop culture (hot rods, tatoos, monster mags, obscure record labels, Mexican wrestlers, stroke mags, etc.) as well as parodies of famous trademarks of the recent past. In one case we simply appropriated the Edsel logo. • Actually, we all think "logos" are pretty stupid.

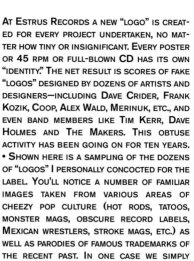

ESTRUS CENTER FOR MORAL ENHANCEMENT

ESTRO-SONIX

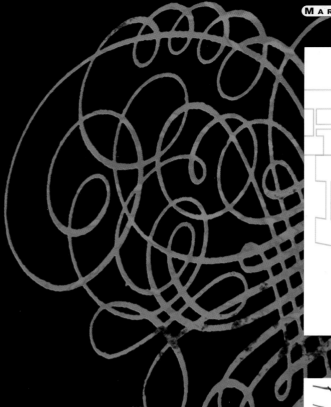

clichÉ cards by margo chase

Hip, Hip, Cliché! Three from a set of six blank cards using well-known clichés as the basis for three-dimensional typographic treatments. Each card includes a description of the meaning and historic sources of the cliché on its back. Size: 5"x 7" / Client: Westland Graphics and Margo Chase Design.

5 favorite fonts:

My taste in type changes about as fast as my taste in clothes. Envision, pterra, bell gothic, info text, and bradley are my top 5 fonts this week. Three of which are my own designs.

poster design by steven r. gilmore / size: 18"x 24" / client: the holy body tattoo / purpose: poster announcing dance performance

(Opposite) These cliché cards would have to qualify as some of my favorite designs because I learned so much in the process of creating them. I've wanted to learn Electric Image and Infini-D (two 3-D rendering programs) for quite awhile, but I never learn software unless I have a reason. So, I tricked myself into learning by creating a project that required me to. I've also wanted to get out of the trap of design as a service and begin a line of products of my own. The idea to use clichés as greetings evolved from my struggle to write original card copy. I enjoy language, but everything I wrote sounded like a cliché, so I decided to go with it. Doing the research into the derivation of these clichés was great fun (and it's made everyone at my studio a much more interesting dinner guest). I also like the fact that these pieces have a sense of humor, which doesn't happen very often in my work. Besides, how often do you get to tell someone to "go fry an egg" in a nice way?

This Holy Body Tattoo poster by Steven Gilmore is definitely among my favorite typographic pieces of the last few years. Steven's work is always amazing, rich, layered and mysterious. He has a beautiful sense of color, and I'll never know where he finds clients who actually pay for stuff this cool.

-margo chase

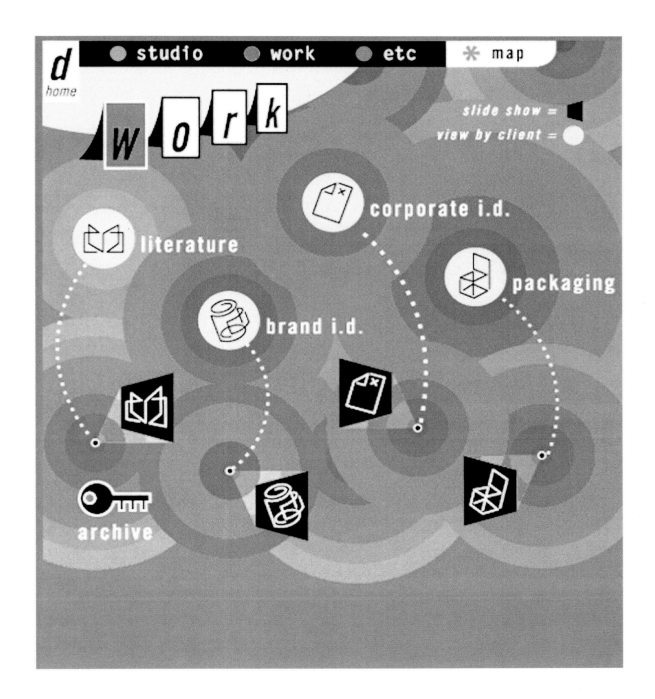

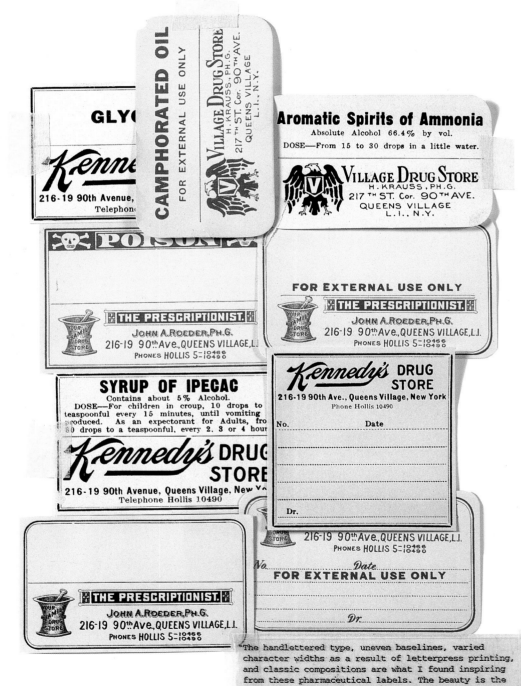

"The handlettered type, uneven baselines, varied character widths as a result of letterpress printing, and classic compositions are what I found inspiring from these pharmaceutical labels. The beauty is the seemingly effortless 'non designed' character they possess."

French Paper Co Parchtone Promotion   Laurie DeMartino

"Choosing a single piece that represents my approach to typography is tough, but I think this promotion for French Paper comes close. I believe type should be used as an aesthetic element that is compatible with the overall concept, as well as to convey information. For this piece, I wanted the type to promote the paper, but also to be useful and (hopefully) entertaining. Although I appreciate many of the typefaces out there today, I find that I actually use very few of them, concentrating instead on varying their applications."

CALL FOR ENTRIES
FOR THE 35 TYPE DIRECTORS CLUB ANNUAL EXHIBITION.

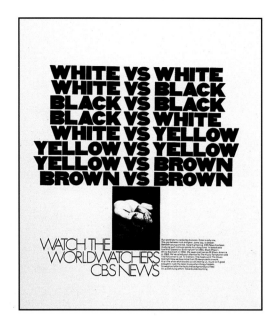

WHITE VS WHITE
WHITE VS BLACK
BLACK VS BLACK
BLACK VS WHITE
WHITE VS YELLOW
YELLOW VS YELLOW
YELLOW VS BROWN
BROWN VS BROWN

WATCH THE
WORLDWATCHERS
CBS NEWS

Innovation: Washington.
Initiation: Paris.
Indication: Saigon.
Intensification: Hanoi.
Indoctrination: Peking.
Inflammation: Prague.
Indignation: Moscow.
Imputation: Tel Aviv.
Implication: Cairo.
Intervention: U.N.
Installation: Grand Forks.
Investigation: Moon.

WATCH
THE WORLDWATCHERS
CBS NEWS

This is a campaign which I created, wrote, and designed for CBS News some years ago (you can gauge by the headlines). The typographic variation reflects the news subject in each ad. The purpose of the campaign was to underscore the scope of CBS news coverage here and abroad. The campaign ran nationally and local CBS station call letters were added in each market. The halftones in the signatures were frames from my TV commercial about the "CBS Worldwatchers," a signoff created for the news department.

Onofrio Paccione, who ranks as a top creator, conceiver, designer, art director, typographer—and more recently, a painter—created the poster for the New York Type Directors Club. His concept, design, photography, and type are all evident.

Collision at Columbia,
Backfire at Berkeley,
Strife at Sorbonne,
Disruption at Duke,
Opposition at Oxford,
Semantics at San Francisco,
Turmoil at Tokyo,
Conflict at Chicago,
Revolt at Rutgers,
No nonsense at Notre Dame.

WATCH
THE WORLDWATCHERS
CBS NEWS

Nixon watches Kosygin.
Kosygin watches Mao.
Mao watches Ho.
Ho watches Ky
(Who watches Thieu).
Nasser watches Dayan.
Dayan watches DeGaulle.
DeGaulle watches Nixon.
Cronkite watches Everybody.

WATCH
THE WORLDWATCHERS
CBS NEWS

ABM, NLF, DMZ, SAM,
LEM, HEW, DEW, FCC,
LSD, DNA, HRA, UAR,
HUD, FTC, CIA, AMA,
ABA, OEO, FDA, SDS,
SOS!

WATCH
THE
WORLDWATCHERS
CBS NEWS

Some of the best type solutions are those that come from the designer's own hand.

Rendered type, calligraphy or "found art" can often be the best ways of expressing the emotion of the material.

twenty-three countri...
...e world have low...
...ortality rates than...
...nerica," says Fallo...
...unding partner...
...hat's the kind of...
...eeps us dedicat...
...e the Chi...

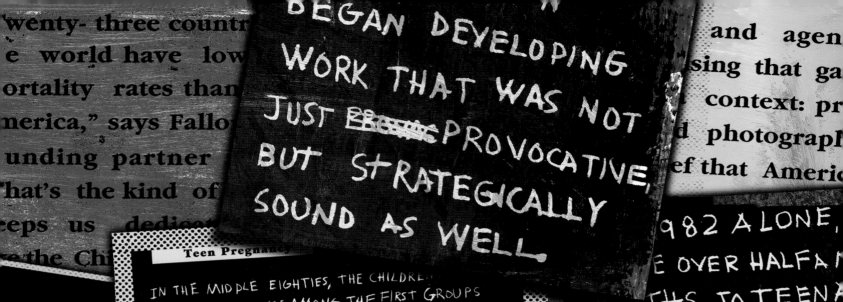

BEGAN DEVELOPING
WORK THAT WAS NOT
JUST ~~PROVO~~ PROVOCATIVE,
BUT STRATEGICALLY
SOUND AS WELL

and agen...
...sing that ga...
...context: pr...
...d photograph...
...ef that Americ...

1982 ALONE,
...E OVER HALF A...
...IRTHS TO TEENA...
MOTHERS IN THE...
STATES, THE HIGH...
IN THE WESTERN...
WHAT'S MORE, THE...
KNEW NO RACIAL O...
BOUNDARIES. NO O...
IMMUNE. STILL THE...
BELIEF WAS THAT...
PREGNANCY WAS SOM...
THAT HAPPENED TO:...
ELSE'S DAUGHTER,...
ELSE'S SISTER OR...

Teen Pregnancy

IN THE MIDDLE EIGHTIES, THE CHILDREN
DEFENSE FUND WAS AMONG THE FIRST GROUPS
TO BRING ATTENTION TO THE FAR-REACHING,
NEGATIVE EFFECTS OF TEEN PREGNANCY. THE
PROBLEM HAD REACHED EPIDEMIC PROPORTIONS.

PROJECT CEASE FIRE WAS BORN.

CONGRATULAT...
...UGHT MORE VIOL...
...HAN ABC, CBS, A...

...s the chance of a gun death almost 300%. Which means instead o...

...SHOWED THAT...
...HOME FOR P...
...E LIKELY TO...
...AN UNTRUDER...
...G COULD REBU...
...COULD KEEP...
...NS MIGHT FI...
...ANDS OF CH...

THIS IS HOW MANY SAFE...
REGULATIONS OUR GOVERN...
IMPOSES ON THE PRODU...
THAT KILLS OVER 5,000...
AMERICAN CHILDREN A YEA...

Putting Down the Gun

WITH THE NINETIES CAME   A GROWING AND V...
IMMEDIATE   THREAT TO THE HEALTH OF AMERIC...
CHILDREN. OVER JUST THE LAST DECADE, THE NUM...
OF CHILDREN.   KILLED BY GUNFIRE HAS DOUB...

AFTER
TALKING
EVERYONE
TO
EDUCATORS
TO
FROM
EMBERS,
GANG
AND ITS
THE AGENCY
...CLIEN...

...WITH A...
...OOPERA...
...ULD BEC...
...ALLMARK...

COVER OF A CATALOGUE PRESENTING THE WORK OF SUSAN **COHN** A JEWELLER/ARTIST. THE DESIGN REFERS TO THE ICONOGRAPHIC QUALITIES OF THE WORKS: DONUTS, PERFORATIONS AND GRID. **GARRY EMERY**

c h n

"He looked down
at it slantendicular,
'So,' says he, 'This is all
brimstone but the concept
and
that is aquafortis?'

'It's a ripstaver,'
says I,
'if it ain't, I
wish it may be tetotaciously exfluncated!'

He riz up and put it
to me mighty droll ;

'Feller,'
says he,
'you have spilled the form.'"

CAL ARTS
GRAPHIC DESIGN PROGRAM
SPRING 1993
LECTURE
SERIES
PRESENTS:
A SLIDE
LECTURE
THURSDAY AT 10:30 A.M.
ON MARCH 18th.
IN THE BIJOU THEATER
BY VISITING
GRAPHIC DESIGNER
MIKE FINK

This is part of my series of announcements designed and self-published after the fact (the event). The subjects are designers who lecture at CalArts. While all the information concerning the event (time, place, venue, etc.) is used (and readable!), the "style" of the designer is not, and is about something else (anything other than the designer's work!). In the case of this piece it's the name of the designer, Mike Fink who practiced in Los Angeles. The "wrong" Mike Fink is the Western figure who figured in the Davy Crockett legend and died in 1823 and was know as the "keel-boat king." In this case you must know who the "wrong" Mike Fink was, and how he died and the language used in the early 19th Century American frontier for a kind of ritual bragging and the use of "Americanisms" added to the "King's English." The "typeface" used on this is the hand drawn version of what became "Out West," which was originally done for *Design Quarterly* magazine. Favorite Typefaces: lettering on paintings and photographs, commercial artists' lettering during teens and 20s in America, lettering on buildings in old Western photos, lettering "outsider" artists use on their paintings and objects, the lettering professional sign painters use in the rural and small town environments

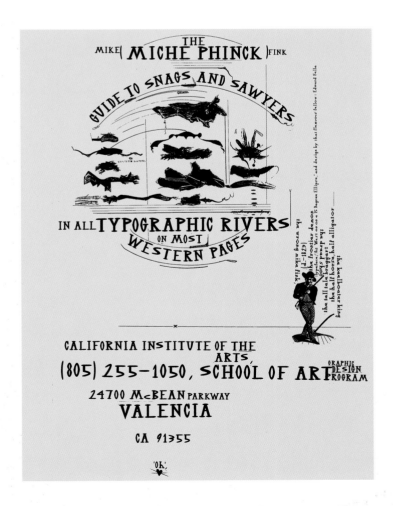

Zeke and Ned book jacket
Designer: Chip Kidd
Art Director: Jackie Seow
Publisher: Simon & Schuster

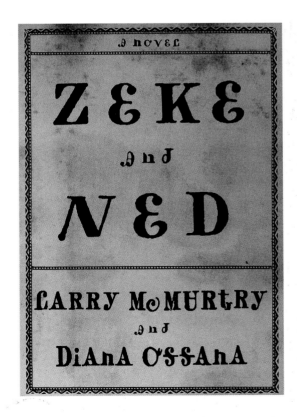

Opposite: Design by Alan Kitching chosen by Alan Fletcher

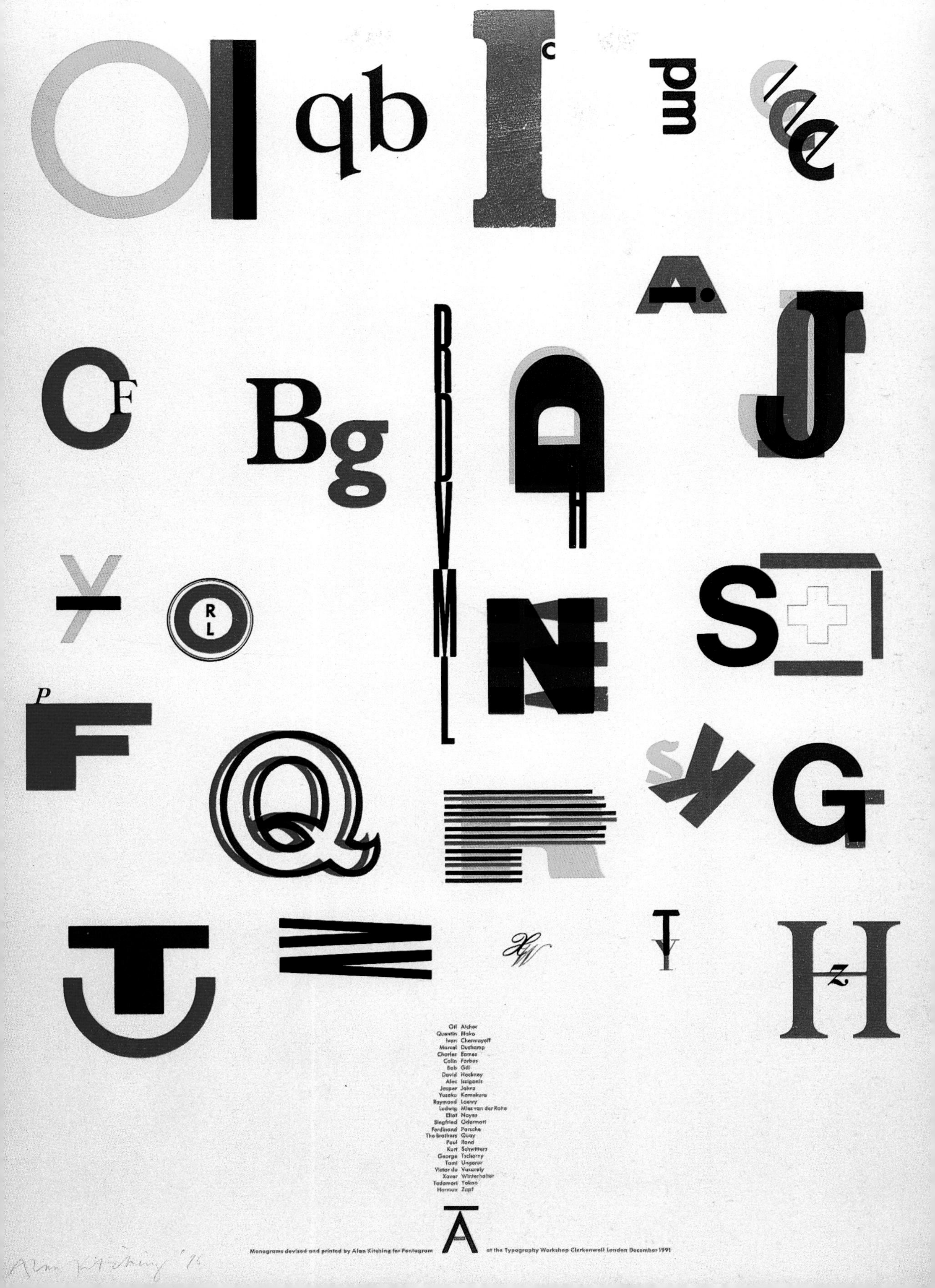

qb

pm

Otl Aicher
Quentin Blake
Ivan Chermayeff
Marcel Duchamp
Charles Eames
Colin Forbes
Bob Gill
David Hockney
Alec Issigonis
Jasper Johns
Yusaku Kamekura
Raymond Loewy
Ludwig Mies van der Rohe
Eliot Noyes
Siegfried Odermatt
Ferdinand Porsche
The Brothers Quay
Paul Rand
Kurt Schwitters
George Tscherny
Tomi Ungerer
Victor de Vasarely
Xaver Winterhalter
Tadanori Yokoo
Herman Zapf

Monograms devised and printed by Alan Kitching for Pentagram   at the Typography Workshop Clerkenwell London December 1991

dal 1° luglio 1996

Centro servizi
ai cittadini
e alle imprese

Milano
11/12 galleria
Vittorio Emanuele

progetto sperimentale

Comune di Milano
Regione Lombardia
Camera di Commercio
Stet Telecom
Ministero delle finanze
Ministero del tesoro
Inps Inail

My favorite
typefaces:

Futura Light
Futura Book
Futura Regular
Futura Bold
Futura ExtraBold

A. G. Fronzoni
was born 1923 in Toscana.
He is as well a museum
and exhibition architect as
an industrial and graphic-
designer.
His first works are dated
back to 1940. From 1967
to 1988 he has worked as
a designer, architect and
teacher in Milano, Monza
und Urbino.
His works can be found in
all major museums in any
part of the world.
In 1982 he founded his
private design-school in

I choose this poster
because it's the most
recent poster i did for
the city of Milan.

I found it an interesting
experiment to translate
my "paper" poster into
a "virtual" interactive
application.

(Right) Here you see some
sequences designed by:
72 dpi,husmann &
benincasa from Milan.

AUG96-FEB97

4TH ESTATE

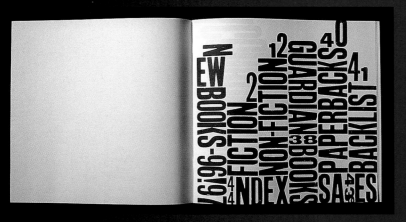

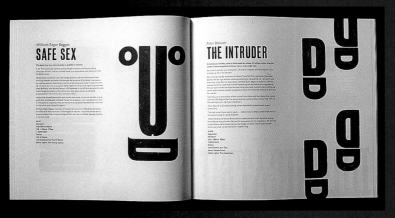

(Opposite) Designing and producing this catalogue for Fourth Estate is the latest piece of work that gave me a real buzz. The whole catalogue was printed hot metal and wood type, and took five solid weeks to print. It was one of those oportunities were the client said 'do what you want' and was trusting and patient enough with me to make it happen.

Spec
Gill sans monotype text 10/14pt hot metal
Various wood type for main illustrations

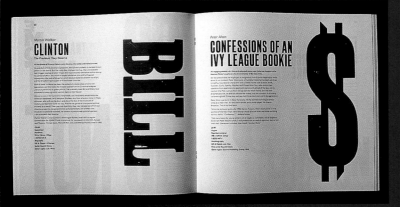

Alan Fletcher's "Michele" knocked me out the first time I saw it. It's one of those ideas that makes you think, 'Why didn't I think of that?'"

MICHĒLE

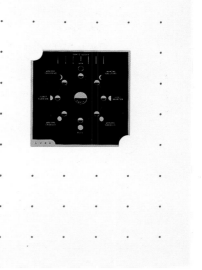

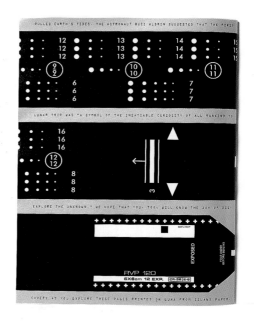

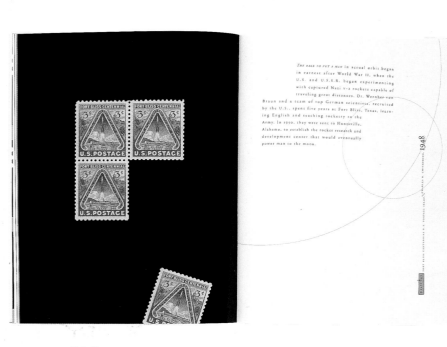

THE RACE TO PUT A MAN in actual orbit began in earnest after World War II, when the U.S. and U.S.S.R. began experimenting with captured Nazi v-2 rockets capable of traveling great distances. Dr. Wernher von Braun and a team of top German scientists, recruited by the U.S., spent five years at Fort Bliss, Texas, learning English and teaching rocketry to the Army. In 1950, they were sent to Huntsville, Alabama, to establish the rocket research and development center that would eventually power man to the moon.

Moonshots is a book we recently produced for Vancouver, B.C.-based E. B. Eddy Paper to promote its number two coated paper stock, Luna. Tracing man's attempts through time to record the moon and the heavens, the book incorporates a variety of images from early astronomical drawings to present-day photography. In keeping with the mix of historical and scientific references, we carried out the orbital theme using a contemporary mix of classic typography and analog line elements.

For as long as I can remember, I've been intrigued by the visual presentation of technical information. I suppose this affinity is the result of some repressed genetic impulse: my father is an engineer. While I don't pretend to understand the content of certain technical books, I do appreciate the order, detail and elegance of their appearance.

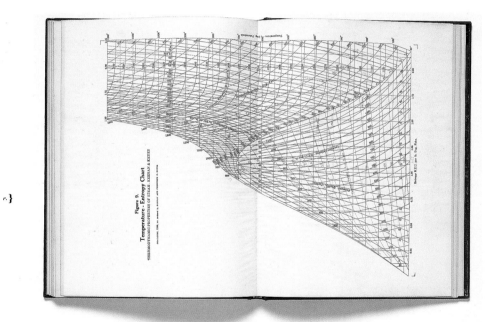

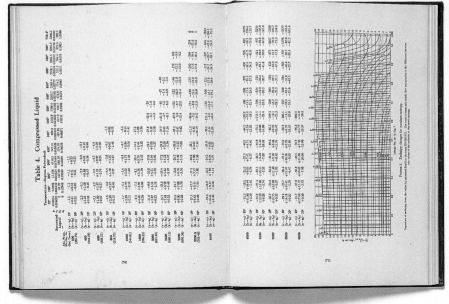

Opposite: This poster was designed to be desplayed in art colleges throughout the UK. It carries information about a special package for students wishing to sub- scribe to *Creative Review* magazine. The first layer is divided into postcards which can be separated and sent back to the publisher.

Vernacular Pieces

I find typographic tools as interesting (and inspiring) as the results they create. Here are two picked up during travels:
(above) 20 mm stencil pack. Torino 1987.
(left) Box of rubber alphabet stamps. Barcelona 1990.

Favorite Typefaces: Bodoni (Bauer), Univers, Franklin Gothic, Frutiger, OCR-B

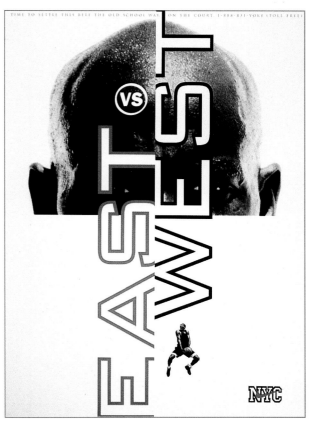

East vs. West

Nike's "East vs. West" is the latest extension of its "NYC" and "LA" campaign which celebrates the differences of the inner-city game, its courts and their heroes on each respective coast. The two examples across the top was the teaser campaign which appeared side by side on the streets of New York and Los Angeles. The typographic juxtaposition of the words East and West in bank gothic type helped to create a split screen effect which was prominent in subsequent executions in print and television. The bottom two examples feature a current street "legend" from each coast and were used as print ads, outdoor and wildposting.

Art Director: John C Jay
Copywriter: Jimmy Smith
Photographer: John Huet
Agency: Wieden & Kennedy
Client: Nike

His name's Predator. Follow him into the paint, and you'll join the 6-feet-under league.

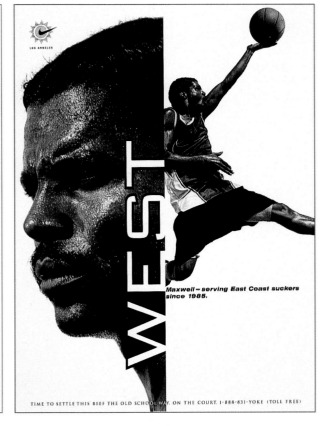

Maxwell – serving East Coast suckers since 1985.

ABCDEFGHIJKLMN
OPQRSTUVWXYZ

ABCDEFGHIJKLMN
OPQRSTUVWXYZ

abcdefghijklmn
opqrstuvwxyz
1234567890

!@#$%&*()_+
-··¢¢£™ıœΣ®†¥¨øπ"'æ...
¬˚∆˙©ƒ∂ßåΩ~ç√∫˜µ≤≥÷

KAMPA DESIGN

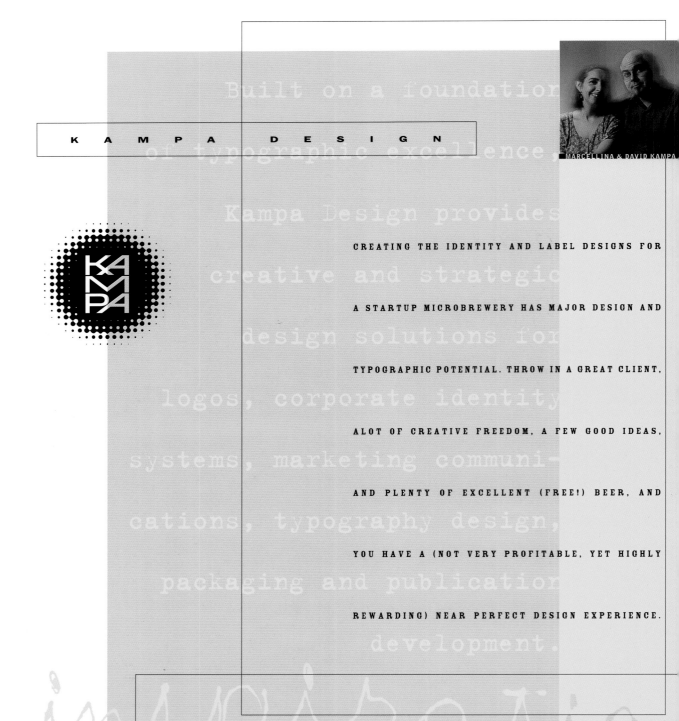

MARCELLINA & DAVID KAMPA

Built on a foundation of typographic excellence, Kampa Design provides creative and strategic design solutions for logos, corporate identity systems, marketing communi- cations, typography design, packaging and publication development.

CREATING THE IDENTITY AND LABEL DESIGNS FOR

A STARTUP MICROBREWERY HAS MAJOR DESIGN AND

TYPOGRAPHIC POTENTIAL. THROW IN A GREAT CLIENT,

ALOT OF CREATIVE FREEDOM, A FEW GOOD IDEAS,

AND PLENTY OF EXCELLENT (FREE!) BEER, AND

YOU HAVE A (NOT VERY PROFITABLE, YET HIGHLY

REWARDING) NEAR PERFECT DESIGN EXPERIENCE.

This is one of my favorite pieces by our son Derek.
I keep it over my computer as a source of inspiration.
At an early age, he began to embellish letterforms
and incorporate words and letters into his drawings.
This pure uninhibited expression has helped me better
understand my own natural instincts toward design.—DK

The majority of our work consists of logos and custom lettering, so we usually create our own type or manipulate existing fonts. We use a lot of Franklin Gothic and Garamond, but that doesn't accurately represent the typographic personality of Kampa Design. Currently it seems we are going through an old-style font phase using fonts like Copperplate, Poplar, Truesdell, Stymie Bold Condensed and Rosewood Fill. Other fonts like Trixie, Dogma and Grotesque Black also show up from time to time.

Traditional beer icons, custom lettering and old woodblock style type gives the Live Oak Brewing Company logo and labels an old-world, hand-crafted appeal.

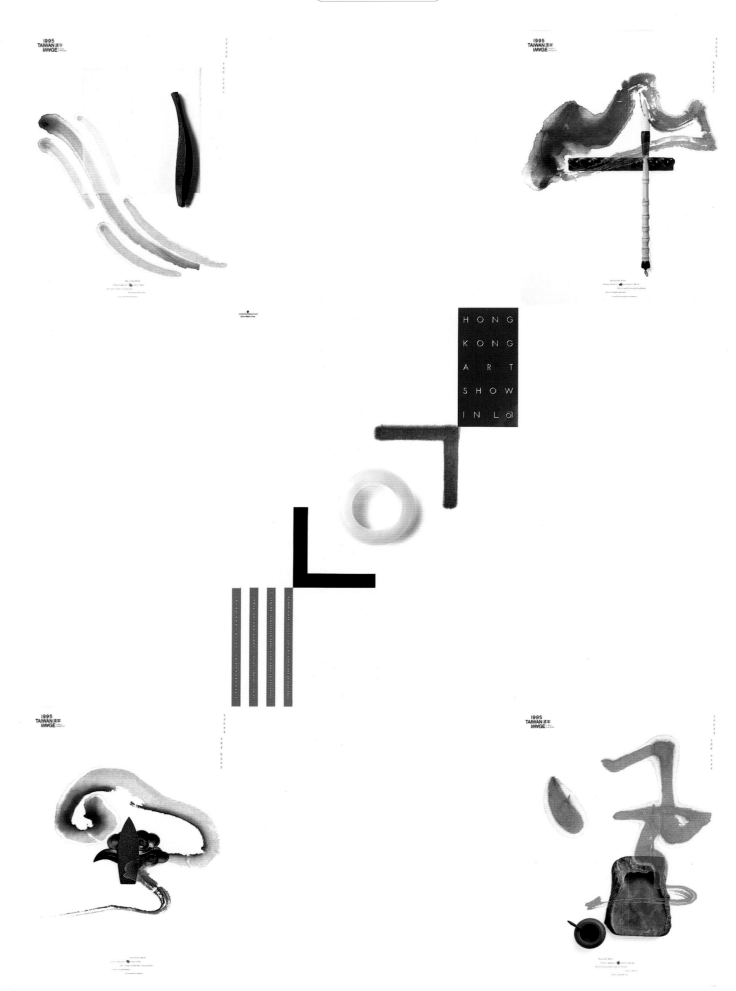

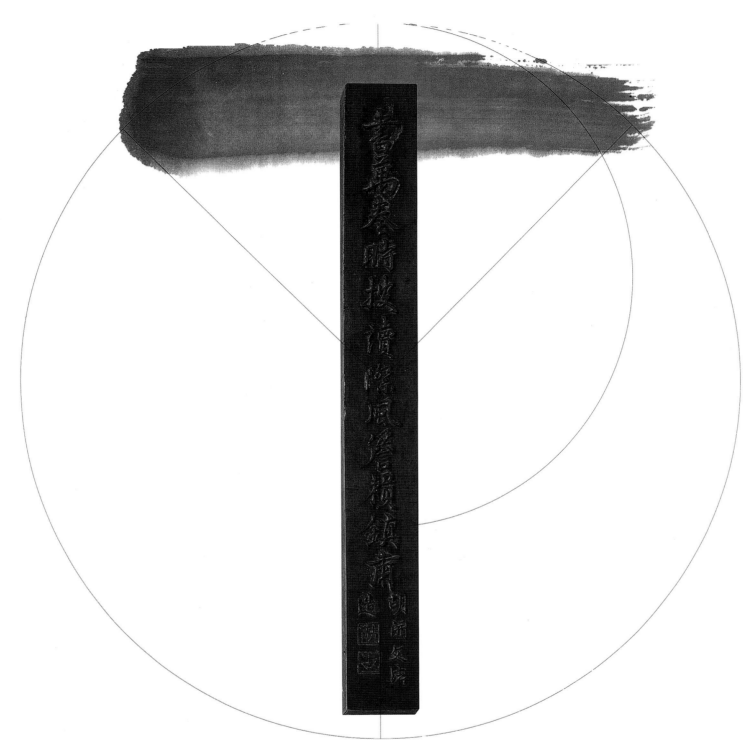

ON THE THRESHOLD OF THE 21ST CENTURY
THE ESSENTIAL ROLE OF TYPOGRAPHY

KAN TAI-KEUNG

Conceived, organized, and with an introduction by

HASKELL F. NORMAN, M.D.

———

Catalogue edited by Hope Mayo

———

Based on an exhibition held at

THE GROLIER CLUB

20 September – 23 November 1994

ONE
HUNDRED
BOOKS
FAMOUS
IN
MEDICINE

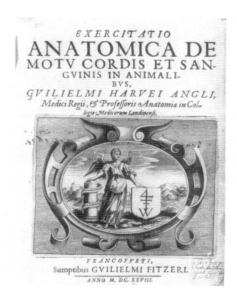

27
———

WILLIAM HARVEY
(1578–1657)

A] *Exercitatio anatomica de motu cordis et sanguinis in animalibus.*
Frankfurt: Sumptibus Guilielmi Fitzeri, 1628.

4º: A–I⁴ K². 38 leaves, pp. *1–2* 3–72 [4]. Engraved title vignette; 2 engraved plates. Quire K, the errata, is not found in all copies.

GM 759. *Heirs of Hippocrates* 416. Horblit 46. Keynes 1. Krivatsy 5328. Norman 1006. Osler 692. PMM 127. Waller 4088. Wellcome 3069.

B] GIROLAMO FABRICI (ca. 1533–1619). *De venarum ostiolis.*
Padua: Ex typographia Laurentij Pasquati, 1603.

2º: π1 A⁴ B–C² D⁴. 13 leaves, pp. [2] 1–23 [1]. Tab. I–VIII: 7 full-page engraved plates and 1 double engraved plate (Tab. II), printed on rectos or versos of letterpress pages.

GM 757. Krivatsy 3831. Norman 750. Waller 2886.

Of all books in the history of medicine, none has interested scholars more than William Harvey's *De motu cordis*. Fielding Garrison claimed that Harvey's "work has exerted a profounder influence upon modern medicine than that of any other man save Vesalius."[1]

Born in Folkestone, Kent, England, in 1578, Harvey studied at Cambridge and at the University of Padua in Italy, where he was a pupil of Girolamo Fabrici. He began practicing in London in 1602. Harvey's pioneering physiological observations, gathered from dissections and animal experiments, were first reflected in his Lumleian lectures at the Royal College of Physicians of London in 1616; these included a summary of his early thoughts on the movements of the heart and blood. Harvey continued his researches and in 1628 published *De motu cordis*, which included his revolutionary theory of the circulation of the blood.

The most significant and certainly the most famous of Harvey's observations was his claim that blood moved around the body in a circle—propelled by the heart through the arteries and returning to this central organ through the veins. As important as this single discovery was, however, Harvey's book also has a broader significance as an influential example of the value of the experimental method. It was, in the opinion of the historian H. P. Bayon, "the first record of a complete biological investigation" in which a problem was defined, methods to solve it expounded, and the results reported.[2]

[103]

INTRODUCTION

THE 1958 GROLIER CLUB exhibition, One Hundred Books Famous in Science, curated by Harrison D. Horblit (Grolier Club Member 1947–1988) did much to stimulate the collecting of rare books in the history of science. Inclusion of a "book" in this exhibition (and later in the 1964 catalogue) gave the item an official sanction, and was no doubt responsible for the increased prices and demand for items which previously had been more or less neglected. Even those who might have publicly frowned upon the use of lists as a guide for collecting wanted to include Horblit's "high spots" in their libraries. For example, the Houghton Library catalogue of selected acquisitions for 1942–1967 indicated that the Harvard Library "already possessed 106 of the titles he [Horblit] described—an agreeable paradox explained by the fact that, counting alternates, the Horblit list actually contains 130 books."[1]

Josiah K. Lilly, Jr. (Grolier Club Member 1928–1966), whom David A. Randall (Grolier Club Member 1944–1975) described as "the *beau idéal* of the perfect collector" decided after World War II to collect, among others, classic books in the history of medicine and science from the beginnings to the present time. Lilly, who liked to collect from lists such as the Grolier "One Hundreds" of American and English Literature, A. E. Newton's "One Hundred Good Novels," and Asa Don Dickinson's *One Thousand Best Books*, did not know of anything comparable at the time in medicine and science, and therefore set out to create his own list. He asked W. R. LeFanu, librarian of the Royal College of Surgeons, to compile "Two Hundred Key Books in the History of Medicine and Surgery," and Professor I. Bernard Cohen, then managing editor of *Isis*, to do the same for science. David A. Randall, the eminent book dealer and later Lilly librarian, wrote that Lilly's interest in lists was not because he lacked imagination but rather that he used them as springboards from which to begin his collection.[2] Neither the LeFanu nor the Cohen list was ever published. W. R. LeFanu advised me that plans were made in the early seventies to publish the medical list with descriptions and bibliography, but this project was later limited to books in the Lilly Library and published in 1976 as *Notable Medical Books*.[3]

Lists and exhibitions such as these limit their total entries to round numbers—ten, twenty, one hundred, two hundred, or one thousand—in part because these figures seem to possess magical qualities. Bern Dibner (Grolier Club Member 1957–1979), referring in the preface of his *Heralds of Science* to his choice of two hundred, said, "This magic is of no more importance than a landing in a long staircase. It is a stopping point at which one can pause, catch one's breath, and look around."[4] We, like Harrison Horblit, have followed the Grolier Club tradition of one hundred. We understand that there has been some criticism of Horblit for not limiting himself to precisely that number, since occasionally he added, in subordination to some entries, other books which served to introduce, amplify,

[ix]

ABBREVIATIONS

ABRAMS
Paul Needham. *The George Abrams Collection*. Sotheby's London, 16 November 1989.

ADAMS
H. C. Adams. *Catalogue of Books Printed on the Continent of Europe, 1501–1600, in Cambridge Libraries*. 2 vols. Cambridge, 1967.

AHMANSON-MURPHY
A Catalogue of the Ahmanson-Murphy Aldine Collection at UCLA. Compiled by Nicolas Barker, et al. Los Angeles, 1989–.

AUSTIN
Gabriel Austin. *The Library of Jean Grolier: A Preliminary Catalogue*. New York, 1971.

BAL
Bibliography of American Literature. Compiled by Jacob Blanck; edited and completed by Michael Winship. 9 vols. New Haven, 1955–91.

BENJAMIN
Catalogue of the Medical History Collection Presented to UCLA by Dr. and Mrs. John A. Benjamin in Honor of Bennet M. Allen and Boris Krichesky. Los Angeles, 1964.

BISHOP
P. James Bishop. "A Bibliography of Auenbrugger's 'Inventum novum' (1761)," *Tubercle* 42 (1961): 75–90.

BISHOP & GOLDIE
W. J. Bishop and Sue Goldie. *A Bio-Bibliography of Florence Nightingale*. London, 1962.

BLAKE
John B. Blake. *A Short Title Catalogue of Eighteenth Century Printed Books in the National Library of Medicine*. Bethesda, Md., 1979.

BMC
British Museum. *Catalogue of Books Printed in the XVth Century Now in the British Museum*. London, 1908–.

BSB-INK.
Bayerische Staatsbibliothek Inkunabelkatalog. Edited by Elmar Hertrich. Wiesbaden, 1988–.

CHASE
Merrill W. Chase, et al. "The Bibliography of Dr. Karl Landsteiner," *Journal of Immunology, Virus Research and Experimental Chemotherapy* 48 (1944): 5–16; reprinted as "Karl Landsteiner-Bibliographie," in Paul Speiser, *Karl Landsteiner, Entdecker der Blutgruppen: Bibliographie eines Nobelpreisträgers aus der Wiener Medizinischen Schule* (Vienna, 1961), pp. 97–111.

CHOULANT-FRANK
Ludwig Choulant. *History and Bibliography of Anatomic Illustration*. Translated and annotated by Mortimer Frank. New York, 1945.

CIBN
Bibliothèque National. *Catalogue des Incunables*. Edited by Ursula Baurmeister, Annie Charon-Parent, and Dominique Coq. Paris, 1981–.

COLEBROOK
L. Colebrook. "Alexander Fleming," *Biographical Memoirs of Fellows of the Royal Society*, 1956, 2: 117–27.

CRAINZ
Franco Crainz. "The Editions and Translations of Dr. Matthew Baillie's *Morbid Anatomy*," *Medical History* 16 (1982): 443–52.

CUSHING
Harvey Cushing. *A Bio-Bibliography of Andreas Vesalius*. New York, 1943; reprinted, Hamden, Conn., 1962.

CUSHING SOCIETY
Harvey Cushing Society. *A Bibliography of the Writings of Harvey Cushing: Prepared on the Occasion of His Seventieth Birthday, April 8, 1939*. Springfield, Ill., 1939.

DOBELL
Clifford Dobell. *Antony van Leeuwenhoek and His "Little Animals."* New York, 1932; reprinted, New York, 1960.

DOE
Janet Doe. *A Bibliography of the Works of Ambroise Paré*. Chicago, 1937.

DOHENY
Felix de Marez Oyens and Paul Needham. *The Estelle*

[xxxix]

JERRY KELLY

Designer, The Stinehour Press
Proprietor, The Kelly/Winterton Press
Freelance designer and calligrapher

OF THE MANY projects I have been fortunate enough to work on, books relating to bibliographic topics are among my favorites. The Grolier Club in New York has a long, distinguished record of producing important publications relating to the world of fine books. Their series of "One Hundred Books Famous In…", dating back almost 100 years, includes titles relating to English literature, science, and other significant areas. When I was asked to design the latest title in the series, *One Hundred Books Famous in Medicine*, I was delighted. A few pages from the book are shown at left.

A book such as this required, I believe, something of a classic, monumental treatment. I chose the lovely Adobe Garamond type, rendered by Robert Slimbach. Not only is this a beautiful, classic typeface, but it also has myriad peripheral fonts and characters which supplied the various typographic material needed in complicated text such as this.

ADOBE GARAMOND, so well thought out and accurately based on the historic original cut by the Frenchman Claude Garamond in the sixteenth-century, and redrawn by Robert Slimbach, is among my favorites fonts.

I have so many types which I like that it would be difficult to pick the most appealing. In addition to Adobe Garamond I'd include several of Hermann Zapf's types, such as Aldus, Optima, and Michelangelo. Trump Medieval is another favorite, as is Joseph Blumenthal's Emerson design (which unfortunately is only available in metal).

I AM PASSIONATE about fine books, so selecting a favorite work which someone else has produced is difficult, but again I would mention one of Zapf's books. His main publications include *Pen and Graver, Manuale Typographicum,* and *Poetry Through Typography*, but if I had to choose I'd lean towards *Typographic Variations* (1963). This collection of 78 book and title pages shows a breadth of design which is inspiring. The careful composition and meticulous presswork add to the pleasure of the book, to say nothing of the fine binding and paper.

Nel mezzo del cammin di nostra vita
mi ritrovai per una selva oscura,
 chè la diritta via era smarrita.

giorno se n'andava e l'aere bruno

PER ME SI VA NELLA CITTÀ DOLENTE

Ruppemi l'alto sonno nella testa

Canto del cerchio

'Pape Satan, pape Satan aleppe!'
cominciò Pluto con la voce chioccia;
e quel savio gentil, che tutto seppe,

rguitando, ch'assai prima
faremo al piè dell'alta torre,
la nostra m'andar suso alla cima

r che vilta di fuor mi pinse
ndo il duca mio tornare in volta,

Ora sen va per un secreto calle,
tra 'l muro de la terra e li martìri,
lo mio maestro, ed io dopo le spalle.

In su l'estremità d'un'alta ripa
che facevan gran pietre rotte in cerchio,
venimmo sopra più crudele stipa;

Poi che la carità del natio loco
mi strinse, raunai le fronde sparte,
e rendi'le a colui, ch'era già fioco.

Ora cen porta l'un de' duri margini;
e 'l fummo del ruscel di sopra aduggia,
sì che dal foco salva l'acqua e li argini.

Ecco la fiera con la coda aguza,
che passa i monti e rompe i muri e l'arm
ecco colei che tutto il mondo appuzza!'

Luogo è in inferno detto Malebolge,
tutto di pietra di color ferrigno,
come la cerchia che dintorno il volge.

O Simon Mago, o miseri seguaci
che le cose di Dio, che di bontate
deon essere spose, voi rapaci

Di nova pena mi conven far versi
e dar matera al ventesimo canto
della prima canzon, ch' e de sommersi.

Così di ponte in ponte, altro parlando
che la mia comedia cantar non cura,
venimmo; e tenavamo il colmo, quando

Io vidi già cavalier muover campo,
e cominciare stormo e far lor mostra,
partir per loro scampo;

Taciti, soli, senza compagnia
n'andavam l'un dinanzi e l'altro dopo,
come' frati minor vanno per via.

In quella parte del giovanetto anno
che 'l sole i crin sotto l'Aquario tempra
e già le notti al mezzo dì sen vanno,

e sue parole si

odi, Fiorenza, poi che se' si grande,
che per mare e per terra batti l'ali,
e per lo 'nferno tuo nome si spande!

Già era dritta in su la fiamma e quota
per non dir più, e già da noi non gia
con la licenza del dolce poeta,

i poria mai pur con parole sciolte

La molta gente e le diverse piaghe
avean le luci mie si inebriate,
Nel tempo che Iunone era crucciata
per Semele contra 'l sangue tebano,
come mostrò una e altra fiata,
Una medesma lingua pria mi morse,
sì che mi tinse l'una e l' altra guancia,
e poi la medicina mi riporse:
S' io avessi le rime aspre e chiocce,
come si converrebbe al tristo buco
sovra 'l qual pontan tutte l' altre rocce,
La bocca sollevo dal fiero pasto
quel peccator, forbendola a' capelli
del capo ch' elli avea di retro guasto.
'Vexilla regis prodeunt inferni
verso di noi; pero dinanzi mira'
disse 'l maestro mio 'se tu 'l discerni.'

Dante's Inferno [*Kitching's italics*]

A poem of thirty-four cantos (c. 1314-1319)
The first stanza from each canto
set in thirty-four founts
comprising the complete set of italic types from The Typography Workshop

(OPPOSITE, LEFT): DANTE'S INFERNO
PRINTED LETTERPRESS AT THE
TYPOGRAPHY WORKSHOP, LONDON
IN AN EDITION OF 20
ON VELIN ARCHES NOIR 250GSM
SIZE: 610 X 850MM

THIS PIECE FUNCTIONS ON VARIOUS LEV-
ELS. THE LARGE WOOD LETTER ALLUDES
TO THE SUBJECT MATTER BY ITS RANGE OF
COLORS AND A SOMEWHAT RANDOM
ARRANGEMENT OF THE INDIVIDUAL LET-
TERS. THE SMALL TYPE, BY CONTRAST,
FLOWS WITHIN A VERY EXACT AND LOGICAL
GRID STRUCTURE DESIGNED TO ACCOM-
MODATE THE STRICT ORDER OF ALPHABET-
ICAL LISTING AND HIERARCHY OF TYPE-
FACES AND SIZES.

IT IS THIS COMBINATION OF TWO
APPARENTLY OPPOSED IDEAS AND THE
INTERPLAY OF MEANING, CONTENT, AND
GRAPHIC FORM WHICH I ENJOY AND SEEK.
THIS INTERACTION IS INCREASINGLY HARD
TO FIND IN THE MASS OF TODAY'S TYPE
WORKS.

(RIGHT) POSTER BY GEORGE MAYHEW
(1927-1966)
I HAVE ALWAYS ADMIRED THE GRAPHIC
WORK OF GEORGE MAYHEW. HE WAS ONE
OF ENGLAND'S MASTERS OF GRAPHIC
DESIGN AND A WONDERFUL POSTER
ARTIST. THIS POSTER FOR THE ROYAL
SHAKESPEARE THEATRE WITH ITS DYNAM-
IC YET DELICATE USE OF TYPE, ILLUS-
TRATES BEAUTIFULLY THE INTERPLAY OF
FORM, CONTENT, TYPE, AND COLOR WHICH
UNDERPINS GREAT GRAPHIC WORK.

FAVORITE TYPEFACES: BLADO ITALIC
(C.1540), CASLON OLD FACE (1734),
FUTURA (1927), MODERN 20 (1870),
POLIPHILUS (1499), WALBAUM (C.1800)

DRAWING OF ALAN KITCHING BY RON
SANFORD, 1997.

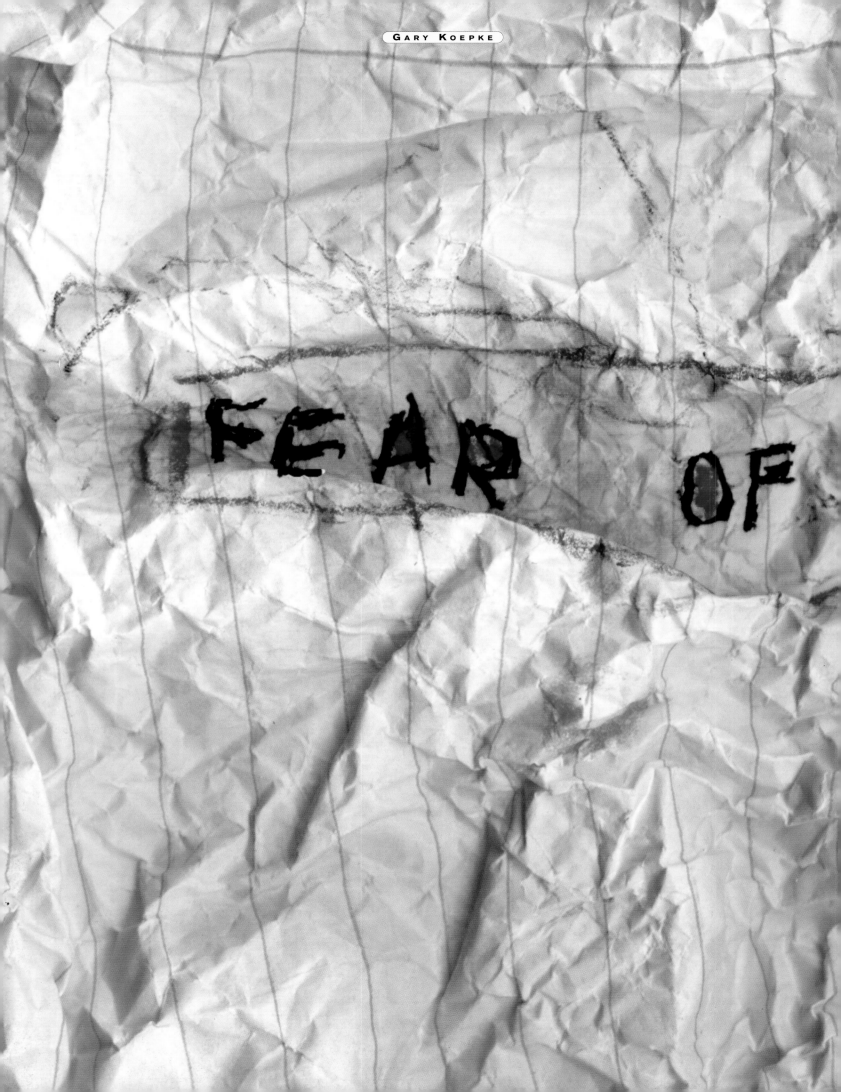

(Above) designs by Toon Michiels chosen by Jacques Koeweiden

劉

LAU

siu–
hong

小康

Hong Kong

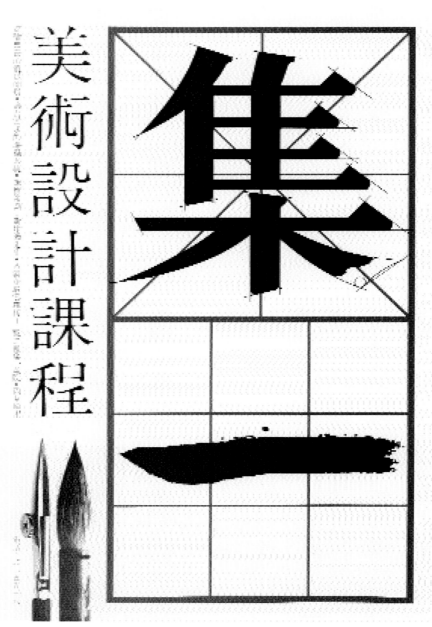

美術設計課程

集一

Design by KAN TAI-KEUNG in 1975

The typeface used on the
poster was designed in Sung
Dynasty (960-1197)
and this poster design is a
combination of typeface and
Chinese calligraphy.
I was a high school student
when the first time I saw this
poster, the Sung Dynasty
typeface used on this poster
let me perceive the beauty
of the Chinese character
design and this influence my
future to study graphic design
rather than fine arts.

天
T I A N A N

china

investments
company limited

A property development
company in China.
The word "天" (sky) is used
to structure a simple
symbol which resembles
a Chinese doorway
symbolizing China opening
her door to many business
opportunities. The use
of the character "天"
because the Chinese name
of this company is "天安",
and in the Chinese culture,
it means the emperor,
the most powerful leader
in China.

印
P R I M E

publishing
limited

A non-profit group with
an emphasis on the subject
of Buddhism, in which
books were published and
distributed free of charge
to interest parties.
The heart-shaped
Bodhi-tree leaf, a holy
object, contrasting with the
graphic character "印"
revealed the objective of
the group.

文
G O L D E N

culture times

From the Chinese character
"文", the design strikes a
different approach
to traditional film-making.

女
A N J O

cosmetic

A famous cosmetic brand in
China. The new logo composed
of letter [A] and Chinese
character [女].

ANJO

All Chinese characters
are with only one vowel,
may have many different
meanings or expressions,
for example, the character
"天" has the meanings of
the sky, the heaven,
the faith and the emperor.
In my philosophy of design,
applying Chinese character
with modern·approach
into the identity or logo
design may compose the
design in a peculiar and a
meaningful way, create a
more cubic effect,
and to express a deeper
degree of culture.
Moreover, most of the
Asian are able to read
Chinese character and it
helps the designer
to express their ideas
of design.

WORTBILDWORT

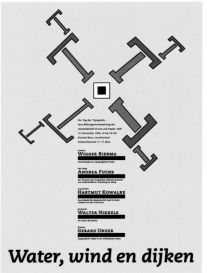

Water, wind en dijken

2
3

1

1 Poster for an exhibition in
Thun, Switzerland, 1990,
for the Type Directors Club
of New York.
Poster size: 90.5 x 128 cm
Typeface: Meridien,
Frutiger
Print: 3-color silkscreen
**2 "A Day for Typography,"
GDP Switzerland, Bern
1994.
Size: 90.5 x 128 cm
Typeface: PMN Caecilia
Print: 4-color silkscreen**
3. "A Day for
Typography," GDP
Switzerland, Zürich 1996
Size: 90.5 x 128 cm
Typeface: Silica
Print: 5-color silkscreen

4-7 Max Caflisch: Versuch
einer Typisierung des
Aldusblattes, Cover and six
pages, 1996
Size: 24 pages, 12 x 18cm

Theo Leuthold, born in
1952, studied with Hans
Rudolf Bosshard at the
Kunstgewerbeschule in
Zurich where he was
trained as a typesetter. In
1990 he founded the
Atelier Theo Leuthold &
Associates, a studio for
information design and
typography, in Zurich. He
lives in Zurich and Amiens,
Switzerland.

Information and Typography. Since 1989 the
Union for Print and Paper (GDP) in Switzerland
has organized "A Day for Typography," during
which professionals in the areas of typography,
design and communications lecture and
present their work.

When I was asked in 1991 to design the
posters for this event, I decided to
experiment with each poster. My idea for
the design for this series consisted
exclusively of lines of copy, typography, and
ink. The large size of the posters allowed me
the opportunity to experiment with the
relationship between reading and looking.
The basis for this was a poster I had
designed for an exhibition of the Type

Directors Club of New York in Thun,
Switzerland in 1990. I had placed the title
and the two lines of information on the
poster in such a way that they formed the
shape of a "T". For this design, I used
Meridien bold and Frutiger bold by Adrian
Frutiger (fig. 1).

"A Day for Typography 1994": The Dutch
speakers Wigger Bierma, Andrea Fuchs,
Hartmut Kowalke, Walter Nikkels and Gerard
Unger spoke on the subject of "Water, wind en
dijken" (Water, wind and dikes). I believe it had
been Gerard Unger's idea as for his own speech
he chose the title "Typographic Hills on the
Dutch Plane." I took up this idea and put a
typographic windmill on the poster, made up

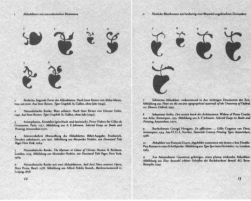

5
6
7

4

by PMN Caecilia in four versions. This was an opportunity to work with Linearantiqua, a very exciting type with emphasis on the serifs designed by the Dutch typographer Peter Matthias Noordzij, (2)

"A Day for Typography 1996": 2 black edge bar elements and above them the colored text lines in Silica regular, semibold and bold. The left-justified text lines come down from three axes. (3) A review Max Caflisch did in the Typographischen Monatsblätter on a new Egyptienne of American type designer Sumner Stone inspired me when I designed this poster. As a designer who does not design typefaces but works with them constantly, I find such reviews most valuable.

A collaboration with Max Caflisch. In 1994 Max Caflisch showed me the first typoscript of his essay entitled Versuch einer Typisierung des Aldusblattes (Experiment in Typifying the Floret) and the images he had retouched. In an introductory essay he follows the traces of this typographic ornament in literature, and in a second part he classifies the historical and contemporary shapes of the leaf, shows its morphology and indicates the sources of the florets. I was fascinated by the subject. I remembered his playful variations of six Granjon arabesques. The essay also appeared as a small brochure. Concerning the choice of typography, Caflisch wrote me

that he prefered Garamond but could also imagine that the Bembo; Poliphilus, Galliar, Sabon or Minion would work well. When I layed out the pages, I realized that when doing the typoscript, Calfisch had already considered a very clear and simple design and how important all parts of the whole are to him. Are the spaces between the words right? Is it possible to include the page numbers without leading close to the type area? Shall the text be printed in red and the ornaments in black? Does the thread stitching of the binding have the same color as the paper? The answers to these design questions were given on October 25, 1996, his 80th birthday (4-7).

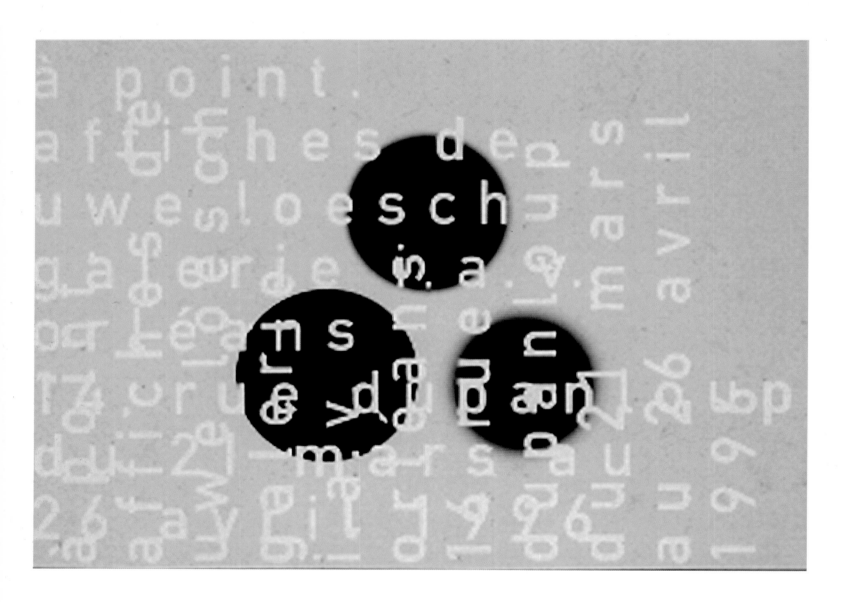

A point: Affiches de Uwe Loesch
Design: Uwe Loesch
Client: Galerie I. A. V. Orleans, France
84 x 119 cm 1996

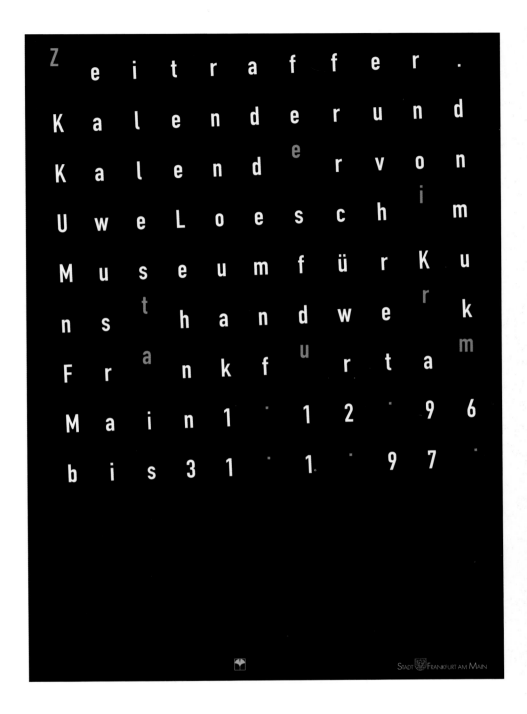

Title: Ta - tan - kah -yo -tan - kah
Hommage à Sitting Bull
Poster for an auction of contemporary art
Designer: Uwe Loesch
Client: PCC Political Club Colonia
each part: 70 x 100 cm 1995

Zeitraffer (time lapse)
Calendars and calendars by Uwe Loesch
Design: Uwe Loesch
Client: Museum für Kunsthandwerk
Frankfurt am Main
84 x 119 cm 1996

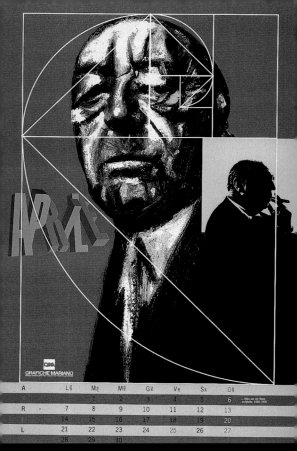

GRAFICHE MARIANO

A	Lu	Ma	Me	Gi	Ve	Sa	Do
		1	2	3	4	5	6
R	7	8	9	10	11	12	13
	14	15	16	17	18	19	20
L	21	22	23	24	25	26	27
	28	29	30				

2 Giugno·Festa della Repubblica

La Repubblica è la casa di tutti

Guardare al passato per vedere il futuro

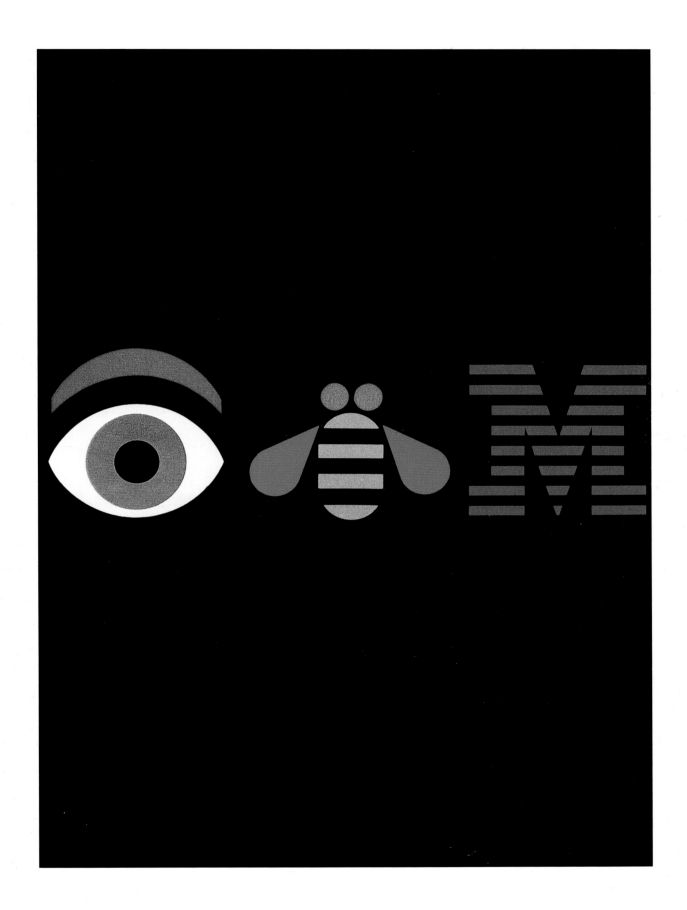

Above: Poster design for IBM by Paul Rand. Chosen by Italo Lupi.

THIS PROJECT—A PAPER PROMOTION FOR APPLETON PAPER COMPANY'S NEW LINE OF PAPER
UTOPIA—IS ONE OF MY RECENT FAVORITES. THE EIGHT-PAGE BROCHURE DEPICTS A
SAN FRANCISCO STREET PERSON'S LIFE STORY AS WELL AS HIS IDEA OF "UTOPIA." THE
HAND-DRAWN TYPOGRAPHY AND COLORFUL MIXED-MEDIA ILLUSTRATIONS SEEMED LIKE A NATURAL
WAY FOR ME TO TELL THIS SIMPLE AND SURPRISINGLY UPLIFTING STORY OF A GOOD MAN. —MICHAEL MAR

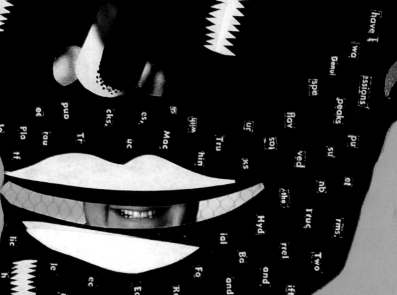

P. SCOTT MAKELA

OUR FAVORITE RECENT PIECE IS THIS PROMOTIONAL POSTER FOR VIRGIN INTERACTIVE,
BECAUSE IT'S ABOUT NOTHING LESS THAN PLEASURE—THE ILLUSION OF PLEASURE.
OUR FAVORITE TYPEFACES ARE DETROIT MM (GILLES, STEPHEN, DAVID FROM ECAL)
BASE (EMIGRE) HUD (MAKELA) WALKER (CARTER) DIN (SPIEKERMANN)

A TWO-DIMENSIONAL
SURFACE WITHOUT ANY
ARTICULATION IS A
DEAD EXPERIENCE

JOHN BALDESSARI
A TWO DIMENSIONAL SURFACE............1967
ACRYLIC ON CANVAS
58 X 67 IN.

(NEED WE SAY MORE?..,..PSM + LHM)

photo CD
presentations
digital printing
menus
postscript
bureau service
colour copies
corporate
repro
Laserbureau
scanning
typese
logos
leaflets
pamphlet
presentations
scanning
retouching
bureau service

As a father of a newborn baby with a liking for daytime screaming, nighttime screaming, and anytime screaming, I subscribe to Alan Fletcher's notion that contraceptives should be used on every conceivable occasion. Part of the attraction of the design is therefore not only its wit, but the fact that it is quite topical. As for the typography I have selected this uncommissioned piece because Fletcher does not bother with any fancy trick which is applied to the idea like custard to apple pie. He has yet to succumb to obscuring the message in favour of some pretty appearance. Instead the message gets straight to your brain without hanging around for too long on the retina. Because your mind is busy smiling about the linguistic acrobatics, it almost forgets to ask why the designer used his personal handwriting and not some beautifully crafted typeface. True to his belief that design is a mental utensil, Fletcher uses words as expressions of observations, thoughts and ideas rather than opportunities to use a typeface.

"You can have all the colours you want, but don't come back with a cool designer solution. I want our logo to tell people what we are doing."
This was Joe Brim briefing me on a new identity for his digital production firm, Laserbureau.
"So what **are** you doing?"
"That changes every four weeks."
The answer to the question – how to create an identity when the company's business keeps changing to stay in line with new technology – is not a logo at all. An eye-catching pattern of the firm's services is applied to stationery, posters, press folders, and even the fascia of Laserbureau's offices. By manipulating colour, pertinent information is highlighted: a name on a business card, a service on a letterhead or a special offer on promotional materials. Like Laserbureau itself, the identity is flexible, plays with colour and thrives on change. As for fonts, the design does not leave much choice. Of the few faces that provide the required ink coverage to create a solid colour pattern, Futura is the preferred option because of its simplicity. One journalist described the solution as "a riot of words and colours, like a carnival in a paint factory."

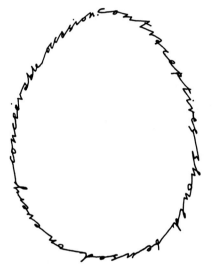

Poster design by Pierre Mendell for an exhibition of architectural photography by Klaus Kinold for the "Neue Sammlung,"
Museum for Applied Art in Munich, Germany, 1995.

John GlaGola

Exhibition of Photography

February 22-29, 1976

Kent Student Center

Kent Ohio

"A poster by my friend Wolfgang Weingart from the year 1976. And it is readable." Chosen by Pierre Mendell.

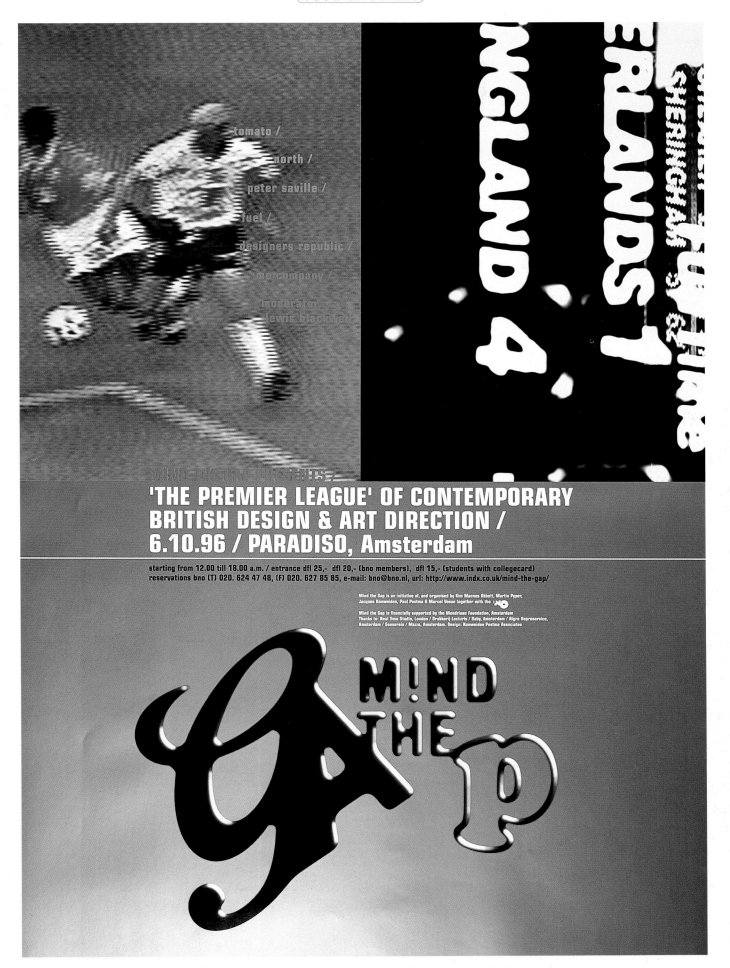

tomato /

north /

peter saville /

fuel /

designers republic /

me company /

moderator:
lewis blackwell

**'THE PREMIER LEAGUE' OF CONTEMPORARY
BRITISH DESIGN & ART DIRECTION /
6.10.96 / PARADISO, Amsterdam**

starting from 12.00 till 18.00 a.m. / entrance dfl 25,- dfl 20,- (bno members), dfl 15,- (students with collegecard)
reservations bno (T) 020. 624 47 48, (F) 020. 627 85 85, e-mail: bno@bno.nl, url: http://www.indx.co.uk/mind-the-gap/

Mind the Gap is an initiative of, and organised by Kim Mannes Abbott, Martin Pyper,
Jacques Koeweiden, Paul Postma & Marcel Vosse together with the bno

Mind the Gap is financially supported by the Mondriaan Foundation, Amsterdam
Thanks to: Real Time Studio, London / Drukkerij Lecturis / Baby, Amsterdam / Algra Reproservice,
Amsterdam / Soeverein / Mazzo, Amsterdam. Design: Koeweiden Postma Associates

M!ND THE GAP

Design by Koeweiden Postma Associates. Chosen by Toon Michiels.

"Type, image, color, and layout are inseparable—readers experience them all at once. The hard work is to make a complex problem look as simple as possible—not to make a simple problem look as complex as possible. Typography is the art of discovering and displaying the fundamental "word-ness" of the story—remembering that, if you succumb to the temptation of overdoing it, you don't display the word, you destroy it. Read the words. It's amazing how often they'll lead you to the perfect typographic solution." —PATRICK MITCHELL

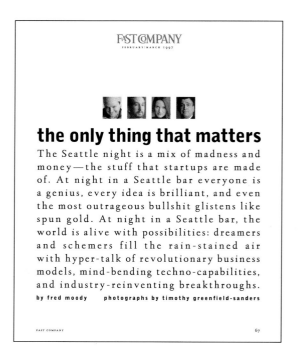

"Typography that transcends the restrictions of 'text' to become an artform. This illustration by Jeffrey Fisher understands the beauty of the letterform."

Stop for one minute and look around. What do you see? Every corporate giant says it wants to change. *Few can do it.* Every young company starts as a natural force for change. *Few can sustain it.* Every organization has people who think they want to be agents of change. *Few can survive it.* Look at each new chapter in the unfolding business revolution of the last 10 years, from Michael Milken's financial engineering to Michael Hammer's organizational reengineering, from corporate restructuring to acquisition fever, from intrapreneuring to startup mania. One dynamic links them all:

CHANGE

BY CHARLES FISHMAN / ILLUSTRATIONS BY AMY GUIP

WATTS WACKER SAYS YOU CAN SEE THE

Article By David Diamond

FUTURE. ALL YOU HAVE TO DO IS LOOK

DIFFERENTLY—AND DIFFERENT. THAT'S

what comes after what comes next

WHY YOU'LL FIND HIM PANHANDLING IN

NEW YORK CITY, RIDING THE RANGE IN

Photography by Everard Williams, Jr.

MONTANA, BUSING TABLES AT TACO BELL.

I WAKE UP EVERY MORNING TO
HELVETICA STARING ME IN THE FACE
FROM QUARK'S DEFAULT STYLE SHEET.
GOD, TAKE ME TO MY DRAWING TABLE,
HELP ME DRAW MY OWN TYPE
AND LIFT ME FROM THIS
CESSPOOL OF FONTS.

(Actually, helvetica's not all that bad.)

– MODERN DOG

"Long live hand-done type! There's nothing like the irregular curves and corners, slab serifs where you least expect them, gentle arcs petering out into misshapen ovals — and knowing these particular things exist only here."

MODERN DOG

Commercial Art Co.

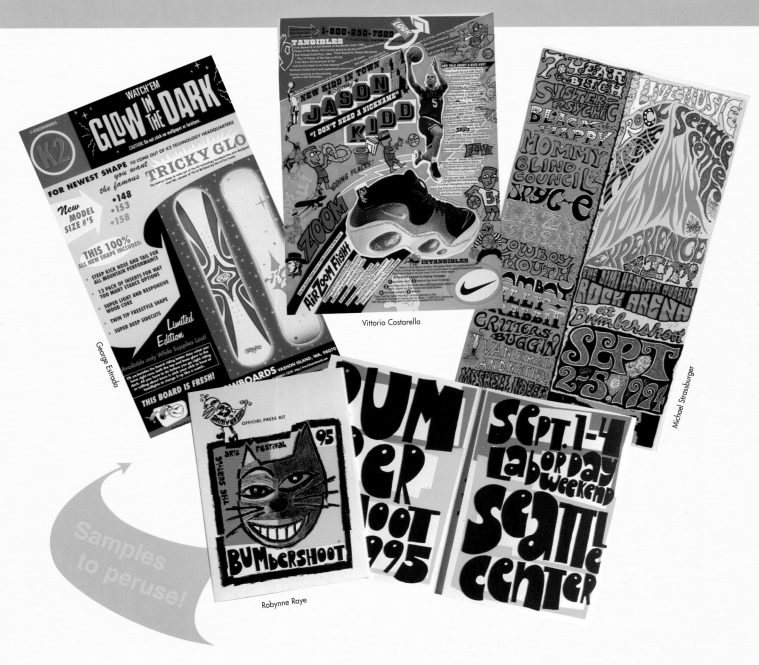

George Estrada

Vittorio Costarella

Michael Strassburger

Robynne Raye

Samples
to peruse!

Gorditos Logo
We love this piece of homespun typography because it is a big part of our personal experience, and it's so charmingly authentic. It's the logo for our favorite Mexican restaurant (the food's delicious and healthy — we eat there constantly). It was created by the owners, a husband-and-wife team. They use this logo everywhere: windows, menus, T-shirts and gift certificates. We like to call it Burrito Bold!

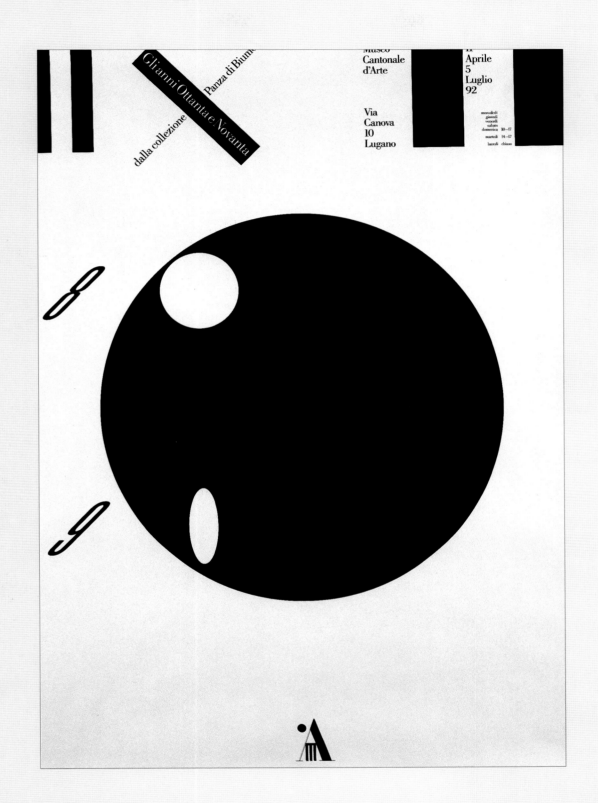

Gli anni Ottanta e Novanta
dalla collezione Panza di Biumo

Museo
Cantonale
d'Arte

11
Aprile
5
Luglio
92

Via
Canova
10
Lugano

mercoledì
giovedì
venerdì
sabato
domenica   10—17
martedì   14—17
lunedì   chiuso

I have chosen three recent
logotypes, each composed
purely of letters. Since they
are logos they must work
very small, and in three
dimensions, and last for
years (hopefully decades),
so this has led me to use
simple forms

Logo for Martin Hamblin,
a market research company
wanting to draw attention to
the benefits of its statistical
techniques

Logo for Designation,
a scheme outlining how
museums can achieve
and maintain high standards
of display

Name and logo for a
management consultancy
which uses training to
help companies achieve
their aims

Letters at play from a children's
book by Kurt Schwitters and
Van Doesburg

A brilliant conjuring trick
for Gebruder Heinemann
by Alan Fletcher

With the merest stroke a letter
is transformed into life blood,
derived from an original by the
Spanish Empire

NOTICE TO CUSTOMERS

This package contains official articles
of Flagstone Brewery.

ALWAYS FRESH. BEST WHEN SERVED COLD.

"First Reserve" is crafted from a unique recipe that
includes a subtle hint of molasses. It's always brewed with
the greatest care, from the finest, freshest ingredients.

Section 1 (a): every bottle of First Reserve gives a fair
equivalent for the money paid. (b) not genuine unless
stamped with the First Reserve Flag".

PREPARED ONLY BY:
FLAGSTONE BREWERY,
Winston-Salem, N.C.

FR Article 12

Conceived in an era when kerning was the space between characters and

tracking was what the Indians did, the Pentagram logotype has managed to

remain intact for over 25 years. A modest configuration of the (then modern

now classic) typeface Pentagram Modern, our logotype is still the place to

go for a quick fix and immediate, self-serving inspiration. Favorite type-

faces include: Pentagram Modern, Garamond 3, Bodoni, Franklin Gothic

and Futura.   Lowell Williams, Pentagram Partner.

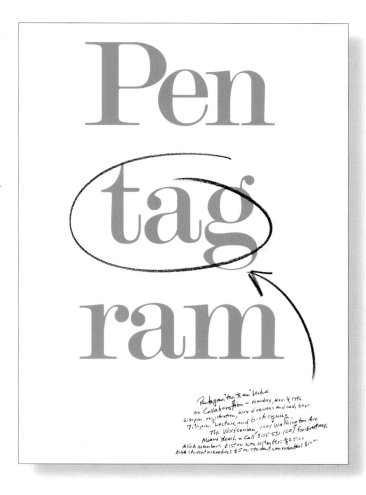

entagram

Far left:
Poster announcement
for partner Michael Bierut's
lecture for the AIGA at the Dallas
World Aquarium.

Design:
Pentagram Austin

Above left:
Poster announcement
for a tag team-style lecture
given by 10 Pentagram
partners in Miami.

Design:
Pentagram NY

Above right:
Invitation to one of several
events commemorating
Peter Harrison's retirement
from Pentagram.

Design:
Pentagram NY

to Jacor and to shareholder value. But knowing when to pull the trigger is as important as knowing where to point the rifle.

As you can tell, we have taken a somewhat unorthodox approach to this year's annual report— providing you with an "audio look" at our stations, our management, and our results during the year. We could think of no better way

to provide you with a profile of the business, philosophy and the personalities that make us uniq

There should be no doubt that 1995 will also be sound year for Jacor. Our strategi are well established and our go is unwavering; buildi value for shareholde When the time right and th opportunities sent themselv we fully inte to pump u the volume.

FINANCIAL HIGHLIGHTS
for the years ended December 31, 1994 and 1993
(Dollars in thousands except per share amounts)

	1994	1993	% CHANGE
Net revenue	$107,010	$ 89,932	19.0 %
Broadcast cash flow	26,542	20,412	30.0 %
Depreciation and amortization	9,698	10,223	(5.1)%
Operating income	13,483	6,625	103.5 %
Net income	7,852	1,438	445.8 %
Per share	0.37	0.10	270.0 %
Capital expenditures	2,221	1,495	48.6 %
Total assets	173,579	159,909	8.5 %
Shareholders' equity	149,044	140,413	6.1 %
Number of common shares used in per share calculation	21,409,177	14,504,527	47.6 %
Outstanding shares	19,590,373	19,499,812	—
Number of shareholders[1]	1,586	1,676	—
Number of full-time employees	568	498	—

[1] Included in this number for each year are shares held in "nominee" or "street" name

Sincerely,

Randy Michaels
President and Co-Chief Operating Officer

2

Let's face it. In the end, typography is meant to be read. Good typography must satisfy three basic challenges: legibility, readability, and aesthetics. To have just one or two of these is considered failure. The 1994 Jacor annual was recorded on a CD as an audio report. The CD was the "hero" and it was important to maintain simplicity around it. But this simplicity is deceptive. The ubiquity of Times Roman, justified into two columns, plays the "straight man" while the illusion of die-cutting through the text is the "punch line." In addition, the reader is rewarded with text that is entertaining and bizarre. No more than a single letter is cut off by the die-cut so that the copy remains perfectly readable. **Robert Petrick, Petrick Design**

Pending protest negotiations with the powerful pedagogues may compel discount investors to boost holdings in diversionary investments such as rock 'n' roll radio, manufacturers of in-line skates for senior citizens, and snow board companies; all this is good news for Jacor Communications, Inc., and considering the fact that Alan Greenspan, in order to combat the tightwad tendencies of an anxiety-ridden yet aggressive investment environment, has announced no further increases in interest rates to ensure positive economic inflation, we can now project film and radio markets will respond positively as ever-tightening cuffs bind Beijing's open-market and systematic abuse of American copyrights which openly and uninventively restrict our nation's corporations from massive capitalistic gains in monetary items resulting from exportation and exploitation and it doesn't take Sherlock Holmes to figure out that the interest in foreign markets that is always waxing and waning within our free market investment community is now waning and this means skittish investors, also in a standard state of non-stagnation, will soon discover a new bullseye which is the manic growth of media madness, notwithstanding the fact that the heavily touted and talked about trend investment in the 90s, the so-called "information superhighway," is still under construction but we are on the expressway with nothing but green lights, gold profits and a glittering horizon as advances in electronics, communication technology and cybernetics hit the pavement running and we sincerely hope that our projections that the radio active commuter population will no doubt expand as taxpayers drop into the disgruntled, disenchanted, non-disclosing

3

The 1994 Progressive annual report is a great example of typography driven by and integrated into the theme of an annual report. It shows playfulness, restraint and respect for the reader as well as the written word, all at the same time. Designed by Nesnadny + Schwartz of Cleveland, Ohio.

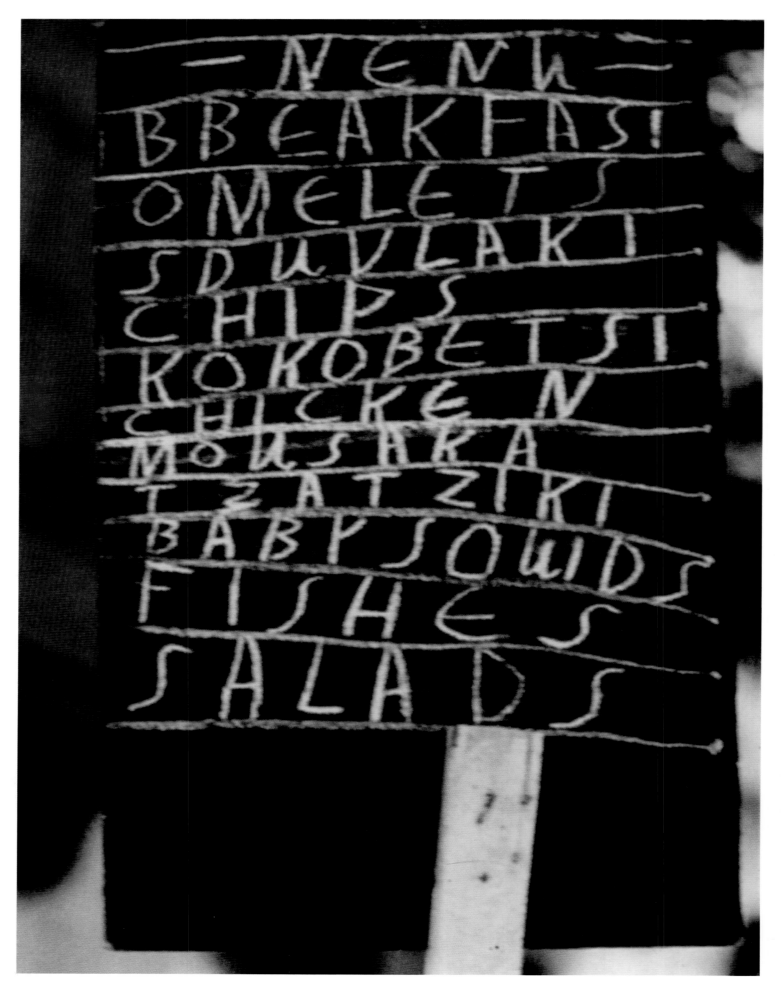

Die feinen
Dinge
entstehen
durch langsame
Arbeit

Chinesische
Spruchweisheit

ein langsames 92!
TEUNEN KONZEPTE gmbh

23/25 R Müller

White

Beckett Papers

Like Jane Porter's description of beauty, it is "the soul shining through its crystal-line covering."

It is us. It is you.

Oh, the mysteries of our own vulnerability!

Who has not looked at a photo of themselves and wondered? Am I

that person?

Is that you? Is me?

The utter **duplicity of our own image:** We think it guards us, enlarges us, paints us on a canvas nobody can see through. But it's simply a magnifying lens for the white heat **glowing inside.**

How can we see so much from so little?

Perhaps the power of a single glance to divulge all secrets is a mystery better appreciated than understood.

My work is inspired by the found or self-produced images that relate to the subject matter of the design. These form the starting point for all my typographical activity.

1
1oo x Foto
Typefaces: Din-Neuzeit Grotesk and Officina-sans

The zeros in the number 100 were replaced by near-circular letters O as a visual pun on the objective view of a camera. The rigid upright typography contrasts with the 'floating' figure in Robert Longo's photograph.

2
Die Meistersinger von Nürnberg
Typeface: Kabel and Akzidenz Grotesk

The organically constructed typography refers to this opera production's set design: an enormous tree made of wooden planks. The diagonal line in the letter e stands at the same angle as the opened beak of the nightingale, king of the songbirds.

3
Wozzeck
Typeface: Akzidenz Grotesk and self-produced typeface

This poster fits in almost seamlessly with the highly graphic set design, which included three-dimensional black houses of various sizes in front of an enveloping yellow backcloth. The typography completes the silhouette of the house, which the soldier and outsider Wozzeck would like to enter.

4
Elektra
Typeface: Monotype Grotesk and Akzidenz Grotesk

The position of Elektra's name opposite the black border signifying mourning emphasizes the isolation and imprisonment of this opera's protagonist. The shape of the letter k – which has been slightly modified – echoes the shape of the axe. The representation of the axe falling in steps refers to the gigantic flight of stairs that dominates the set design.

5
Otello
Typeface: self-produced typeface and Akzidenz Grotesk

The white handkerchief and Otello's black face combine into one image. The face is both foreground and background, while the white and black letters O refer not only to the racial difference but also to the light-giving sun and moon that dominate the set design.

6
Moses und Aron
Typeface: Nobel and Akzidenz Grotesk

This poster – one from a three-part series – is dominated by Man Ray's portrait of Schönberg which has been manipulated. The transparant yellow shape refers to Mount Sinai and the set design. The letters making up Schönberg's name have an iron sheen while his portrait is given a granular rust structure.

The logo of 'De Nederlandse Opera', which I also designed, is featured on all posters in one size and in color contrasting with the background.

Lex Reitsma, Haarlem NL

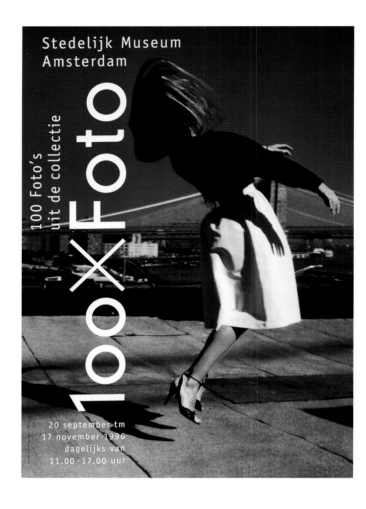

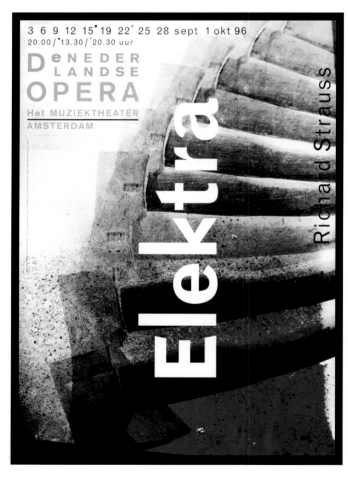

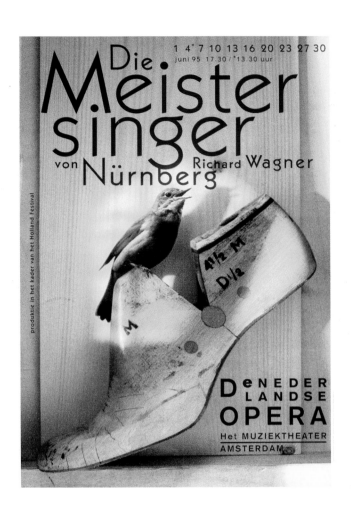

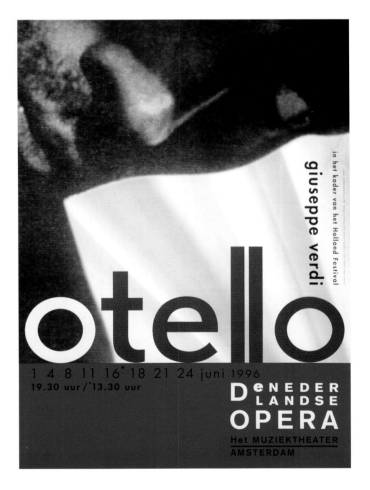

Two of every three corporations doing business today will not exist in 2006.

The survivor[s] will be companies that understand design... and designers who understand what happened.

A company's ideas are its only competitive advantage.

Good design is, at least, the currency of good ideas.

If Jack is a graphic designer and Jack has 12 clients, how many clients will Jack have in 10 years if he continues to work the same way and offer the same services?

11:30am
Friday, October 4

Jack Summerford

Moderating an open-forum discussion on the future of annual reports

According to his contemporary Steven Heller, Jack is "ostensibly a traditionalist whose work, though often underscored by humor, builds upon the basic tenets of modern design while not always representing the old school approach." While Jack's award-winning work has traditionally been corporate communications and identity, he believes that the graphic designer's role is dramatically changing. As he is quoted, "The good designer has always used intellect. It is time we offered our clients more than just paper or plastic."

IBM founder
Thomas Watson
said it:

good design is →

Good design. What makes it "good?" And when it's good, how does it make a business better? Why is it that businesses that do well at design seem to also do better-than-average at

DESCRIPTION: CONFERENCE PROMOTION: TYPEFACES: THESIS/THE MIX 3,4,6 7,8 9 THESIS/THE SANS 4
ART DIRECTOR: LANA RIGSBY DESIGNERS: LANA RIGSBY, JEROD DAME WRITERS: LANA RIGSBY, MIKE NOBLE
TYPOGRAPHERS: LANA RIGSBY, ERIK ADIGARD CLIENT: MEAD FINE PAPERS

Design and the

Bottom Line

CLIENT
Levi Strauss & Co.
San Francisco, CA

DESIGN
Steve Sandstrom
Sandstrom Design, Inc.
Portland, OR

COPY
Mike Koelker
Foote Cone & Belding
San Francisco, CA

(X)

NOTES on RED TAB
LEVI'S POSTER

Part of an extensive point-of-sale, outdoor/transit and print campaign for Levi's developed under the direction of FCB Executive Creative Director Mike Koelker.

The REQUIREMENTS

1. Create awareness and inform customers of Red Tab retailers about the unique qualities of these jeans.

2. Should not degrade other Levi's products.

3. Must be relevant to the Levi's brand – casual, classic, fashionable, cool, and not too hip (for JC Penney).

4. Design must be flexible to work in all media.

5. Must fit into existing Levi's retail shops and merchandising fixtures.

6. Should aim to be collectible.

It takes over 40 separate steps to make just one pair of Levi's Red Tab jeans. With that in mind, "process" seemed to be an appropriate visual direction. Some of the type was hand set. Some was set on a Macintosh. All was distressed and pasted up traditionally on art boards with hand cut overlays. Several versions were printed offset (a) and one version was screen printed and stamped on metal (b).

A BRIEF ANALYSIS of DESIGN for LEVI'S RED TAB POSTER

A. Methodical, mechanical = constructed
B. Orchestrated randomness = natural, casual
C. Imperfections allowed to happen (see B.)
D. Imperfections must be perfect (see A.)
E. Overlapping information = complex = more $
F. Sense of humor (see D.)

LOG — REMARKS / DG ON OR OFF / STANDARD / TIME / DATE / READING / DEV. / READING / DEV. / MAGNETIC HEADING (TRUE ± VAR.) / VARIATION

15—44180–9

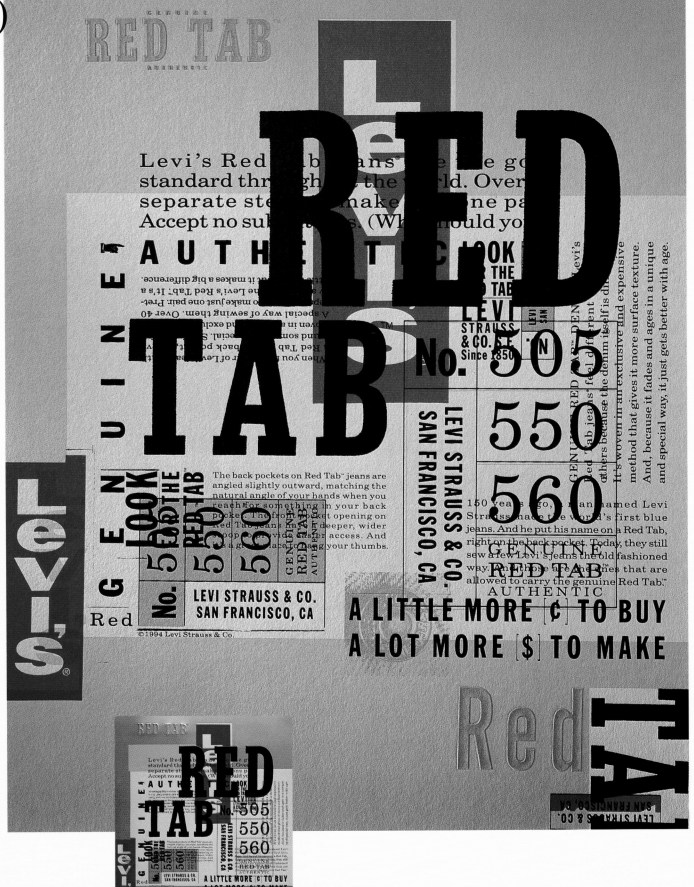

I generally work with typography
to accomplish two goals:
1) to convey information;
2) to convey spirit, mood, personality,
and ideas. I often use type as image,
as these two posters illustrate.
"Art is..." is the verbal slogan assigned
by Silas Rhodes for an anniversary
poster for the School of Visual Arts.
The words are filled with a handwritten
listing of all my favorite artists and
form the typeface "Grotesque."
In the subway, the poster becomes
interactive.

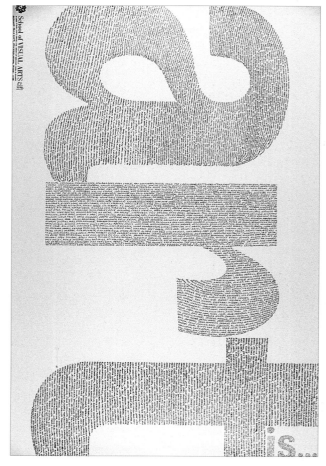

School of VISUAL ARTS

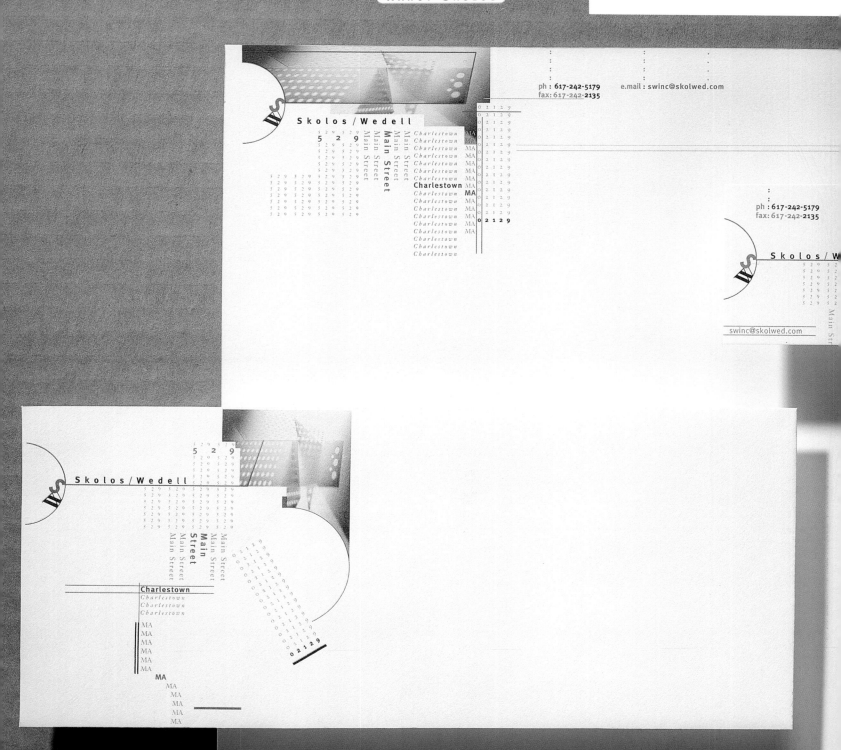

Our studio's
letterhead has
always provided
a wonderful vehicle for research
and experimentation.
We can test things on ourselves
that may not be fair to test on
a client.

recent favorite fonts:

Avenir

Keedy Sans

Matrix

Meta

Rotis

The address was laid out as a map,
diagramming the information as bits
of data within which to locate
ourselves. The original concept was
to list adjacent addresses with ours
in bold. However, that proved to be
too confusing—even for us.

This is our second letterhead since our partner Ken Raynor left in 1990 and we became Skolos/Wedell. Working with "S" and "W," two letterforms that have very little in common visually, was very challenging. After many sketches, I began to see a way to anchor the two letterforms on a semicircle. The rounded forms of the Triplex "S" worked well with the arc of the semicircle. The Bodoni "W" provided a nice contrast and the line weight of the semicircle was adjusted to match the light strokes of the "W."

Our strong interest in
combining typography and
photography was expressed
by the addition of an abstract
photographic image.
The image was created using
frosted acetate with holes
punched at intervals similar
to the letterspacing in the
typography.

V
OI
CI   LA   ?   MAISON
Où NAISSENT
LES   É
TOI   LES
ET LES DIVINITÉS

Ideogram by
Guillaume
Apollinaire
1914

The stationery was influenced by
many typographic models from
the past. The selection of ivory
colored stock with attention to
the texture of the text came
from looking at early printed
books. In contrast, Dada and
early modern pieces were
inspiring for their intuitive,
playful qualities.

Exhibition
Poster by Ilia
Zdanevitch
1922

Erik Spiekermann *et al*   Typedesign @ MetaDesign   1977–1997   Berlin, London, San Francisco

LoType and **Berliner Grotesk** were both designed by ERIK SPIEKERMANN for H. Berthold AG's phototypesetting system between 1977 and 1979, based on hot metal typefaces from the beginning of this century.
A few weights had never been drawn by LOUIS OPPENHEIM (the **LO** in LoType) and the other in-house designers who had been responsible for the original versions, so they had to be *invented* to complement the family. LoType and Berliner Grotesk are now available as PostScript fonts.

FF**Meta** had originally been commissioned by the German Post Office in 1984 for the setting of all their forms, telephone books and other printed matter, which needed to accommodate a lot of very small type on pretty bad paper. What may look overdone and quirky in display sizes, makes the letters and words extremely discernible when used in 8 point and even smaller. That's why FF Meta is at its best when used at those small sizes, and slightly letterspaced at that.
After the German Post Office had decided that they weren't quite ready for the nineties and stuck to their old Helvetica, FF Meta was used as an exclusive houseface for MetaDesign, the Berlin-based design studio – thus the name.
In 1991 FF Meta was released by Font Shop International and has since become one of the most successful faces in the exclusive FontFont Library.

ITC **Officina** was meant to bridge the gap between traditional monospaced typewriter fonts like Letter Gothic and *real* typefaces. It combines the sturdiness required by the impact printer with the elegance of a contemporary face.
This *non-designed* look is considered to be very cool these days, and ITC Officina has been adapted as *the* face for high-tech applications and New Media, including the World Wide Web.
OLE SCHÄFER, typedesigner at MetaDesign, added more weights, small caps and old style figures to ERIK SPIEKERMANN'S original eight versions (Sans and Serif) from 1989.

FF **Info** is named for its purpose: signage systems and information design applications. The weights are carefully designed to compensate for different lighting conditions on backlit and frontlit signs, both with positive and negative text.
As what works in large sizes under difficult conditions also seems to be appropriate for very small sizes, OLE SCHÄFER expanded the original FF Info, based on a design by ERIK SPIEKERMANN from 1988, into a complete family for all purposes.
Three different styles of figures, small caps and arrows are available for all weights of FF Info and FF InfoText. Italics will follow.

ITC Officina

aAAa1223
THESE DAYS PEOPLE NE
ed better ways to com
municate to more diver

aAAa4557
SE AUDIENCES. WE KN
ow from experience
what we have to say is

aAAa6778
MUCH EASIER FOR OTH
ers to understand if
we put it in the right

aAAa9012
VOICE; TYPE IS THAT V
oice, the visible lang
uage linking writer &

aAAa3456
and reader. With tho
usands of typefaces

aAaA1223
available, choosing t
he right one to express

aAilI4557
even the simplest ide

aAaA6998
a is bewildering to m
ost everyone but pra

aAiglI123
cticed professionals

aAiglI456
Familiar images are

FF Info

abilABI123
Ever since people have

abilABI456
been writing things do

abilABI789
wn, they have had to co

abilABI012
nsider their audience b

abiABI345
efore actually putting

FF InfoText

abaAil1213
PEN TO PAPER: LETTERS
would have to look di

abaAil6747
FFERENT DEPENDING ON
whether they were to b

abaAil899
E READ BY MANY OTHER
people in official docu

abaAil0513
MENTS OR INSCRIPTION
s or just one other pers

abaAil678
ON IN A LETTER, OR ONL
y the writer in a notebo

FF Meta

aAAAaA12
PICTURE YOURSELF I
n a world without typ
E. TRUE, YOU COULD
do without some of t

aAAAaA64
HE UBIQUITOS ADVER
tising messages, but
YOU WOULDN'T EVE
n know which packa

aAAAaA53
GE ON YOUR BREAKF
ast table contained
what. Sure enough, t

aAAAAa71
THERE ARE PICTURE
s on them: grazing c
OWS ON A PAPER CA
rton suggest that mi

aAiaA264
lk is inside, and cer
eal packaging has a

LoType

aAbEe123
Stealing sheep? Letter-

aAbE456
spacing lower case?

aAgBe78
Professionals in

aAgBeWy90
all trades, whether they be

aAgBe12
dentists, carpenters

aAeE34
or rocket scien

Berliner Grotesk

aAeEfgHiJ24
tists communicate in la

aAeEfgHiJ13
nguages that seem se

D.J. STOUT HAS BEEN ART DIRECTOR OF THE AWARD-WINNING TEXAS MONTHLY MAGAZINE SINCE 1987. THE MAGAZINE IS BASED IN AUSTIN, TEXAS. HIS FAVORITE FIVE TYPE FACES, ALTHOUGH VERY IMPRACTICAL, HAVE BEEN USED AT LEAST ONCE IN THE MAGAZINE IN THE PAST TEN YEARS. THEY ARE ALL IN THE ROSENBLUM TYPE FAMILY, WHICH CAN BE FOUND IN PHOTO-LETTERING OF NEW YORK'S ONE LINE

IN THE SMALL EAST TEXAS TOWN OF SILSBEE, A GROUP OF BORED AND ANGRY YOUTHS ATTACKED A HORSE IN A FARMER'S PASTURE AND BEAT IT TO DEATH WITH STICKS. ROBERT DRAPER'S FEATURE STORY, WHICH RAN IN THE MARCH 1996 ISSUE OF TEXAS MONTHLY, RECOUNTED THIS HORRIFIC INCIDENT THAT HAD OUTRAGED PEOPLE ACROSS THE COUNTRY. I WANTED TO CONVEY THE PRIMITIVE, BARBARIC NATURE OF THE ACT AND THE FACT THAT IT INVOLVED CHILDREN. I CREATED A CHILDLIKE BUT VIOLENT SCRAWL THAT, IN COMBINATION WITH MATT MAHURIN'S POWERFUL ILLUSTRATION, COMMUNICATES THE VIOLENCE OF THIS

TEXAS MONTHLY · MARCH 1996 · ART DIRECTOR, D.J. STOUT

THE HORSE KILLERS
by ROBERT DRAPER

Bored and angry, a group of kids in a small East Texas town took out their hostility on a horse, whose violent death shook the world.

'CON
NOR

O'Connor has emerged as the decade's first new superstar

SIN
EAD

After weathering some hard and banning losses, Sinéad

ROLLING STONE · JUNE 1990 · ART DIRECTOR, FRED WOODWARD

ONE OF THE THINGS I HAVE ALWAYS ADMIRED ABOUT THIS 1990 ROLLING STONE PIECE IS THE BOLD ALLOTMENT OF VERY VALUABLE MAGAZINE REAL ESTATE ESSENTIALLY TO SET UP THE OPENING TITLE OF THE STORY. NO BODY COPY EVEN APPEARS UNTIL THE FOURTH PAGE OF THE FEATURE. THE PICTURE OF SINEAD O'CONNOR BY ALBERT WATSON, WHICH APPEARS ON THE THIRD PAGE, IS A FINE PORTRAIT BUT ENDS UP PLAYING SECOND FIDDLE TO THE TYPOGRAPHIC PRESENTATION. THE TYPOGRAPHY IN THIS FEATURE IS THE HERO. THIS IS THE FIRST INCIDENCE THAT I CAN RECALL WHERE A SINGLE LETTERFORM WAS SPLIT BETWEEN TWO DISPARATE SPREADS. THIS EDGY TREATMENT OF THE LETTERFORM COMBINED WITH THE STACKING TREATMENT OF THE REST OF HER NAME COULD EASILY HAVE BECOME OVERLY TRICKY AND TRENDY BUT IS HANDLED HERE IN A COMPLETELY READABLE AND CLASSICALLY TRADITIONAL MANNER THAT ENDS UP

90 years

BUILDING ON
PASSION. ART.
ARCHITECTURE.
AND DESIGN: THE
CAMPAIGN FOR CCAC

WHERE THE PACIFIC MEETS THE GOLDEN
GATE. WHERE THE SIERRA CLUB MEETS
SILICON VALLEY. WHERE "MEDIA GULCH"
MEETS THE MUSEUM OF MODERN ART.
WHERE MAKING ART IS PASSIONATE, POLITI-
CAL, PROVOCATIVE, AND POWERFUL...THIS IS
THE PLACE CCAC CALLS HOME.

FOR 90 YEARS, THE CALIFORNIA COLLEGE OF
ARTS AND CRAFTS HAS EDUCATED THOSE
WHO SHAPE CULTURE THROUGH THEIR WORK
AS ARTISTS, ARCHITECTS, AND DESIGNERS.

CCAC IS A PLACE FOR INDIVIDUALS TO FIND
THE COURAGE AND INDEPENDENCE TO
MAKE A LIFE IN ART. A PLACE FOR TEACHERS
WHO PROVOKE AND INSPIRE. AND FOR
STUDENTS WHO TEST LIMITS AND REINVENT
MEDIA. IT IS A PLACE FOR NEW GENERATIONS
OF ARTISTS WHO SEEK TO COMMUNICATE IN
WAYS WE HAVE YET TO IMAGINE.

WE ARE THE CALIFORNIA COLLEGE OF ARTS
AND CRAFTS. AND WE ARE BUILDING ON
THE PASSION THAT LAUNCHED THE COLLEGE
NEARLY A CENTURY AGO.

BIOGRAPHY: ONE COULD ARGUE THAT WAYNE WANG WAS PREDESTINED FOR A LIFE ASSOCIATED WITH THE FILM INDUSTRY.
HIS PARENTS NAMED HIM FOR JOHN WAYNE. HONG KONG-BORN AND CCAC-EDUCATED, WANG IS CELEBRATED FOR BOTH HIS "ART-
HOUSE" AND COMMERCIAL MOVIES. HIS FILMS INCLUDE: CHAN IS MISSING, DIM SUM, SLAM DANCE, EAT A BOWL OF TEA, LIFE IS
CHEAP, BUT TOILET PAPER IS EXPENSIVE, THE JOY LUCK CLUB, SMOKE, AND BLUE IN THE FACE.

PASSIONS: THE CINEMA OF DESPERATION; THE STORIES I HEARD WHEN I WAS YOUNG; MY WIFE'S SOUP AND HER WEIRD SENSE
OF HUMOR.

[CCAC IS LIKE A MOVING PICTURE...] WAYNE WANG. "IF
I were talking to someone who was just starting in film, I would tell them — learn everything, and interdisciplinary work is critical. When I was at CCAC, I took painting from
Phil McKenna, sculpture from Charlie Schmidt, film from Larry Jordan, and photography
from Leland Rice. I learned that painting is much more than oil on canvas. I also went to
school during the Vietnam War era, and I remember all of us — students and faculty —
did printmaking for the anti-war effort. I've never stopped believing that an art school
should be involved in world politics. If I had missed even one of those pieces of my edu-
cation, I wouldn't be able to do what I have done. The most important thing I learned at
CCAC was how to free my mind, to not feel confined to any thing or any medium. When
I look back on those days, I remember I was there 16 hours a day or more. I miss the smell
of oil, linseed, and paint. Most of all, I remember CCAC as a moving picture. When I was
there, I was always changing, always moving. The campus, the teachers, and students were
like that too. I think it's still like that — a perpetually moving picture."

[BORN OF PASSION] PASSION FOR A NEW LANDSCAPE, FOR A NEW
FUTURE, FOR OPPORTUNITY AND SPACE. CALIFORNIA HAS BEEN THE BIRTHPLACE OF DREAMS AND
THE LOCUS FOR REALIZING THOSE DREAMS. FROM THE EARLY 49'ERS TO THE PRESENT INFLUX OF
NEW HIGH-TECH INDUSTRIES, CALIFORNIA WELCOMES THOSE WITH A VISION FOR PROSPERITY, DIS-
COVERY, AND CREATIVITY.

A PASSION FOR FORGING NEW ARTISTIC BOUNDARIES AND A REVOLT AGAINST THE MACHINE-MADE
PRODUCTS OF THE INDUSTRIAL REVOLUTION GAVE RISE TO THE ARTS AND CRAFTS MOVEMENT IN
ENGLAND IN THE LATE 1800'S. THE MOVEMENT, WHICH ENCOMPASSED MANY DISCIPLINES AND
CONSIDERED ART INTEGRAL TO ALL ASPECTS OF LIFE, SPREAD RAPIDLY THROUGHOUT EUROPE AND
ACROSS THE UNITED STATES TO CALIFORNIA, WHERE SOME OF ITS BEST EXAMPLES ARE FOUND IN
THE CRAFTSMAN-STYLE BUILDINGS OF THE SAN FRANCISCO BAY AREA.

CCAC'S FOUNDER, FREDERICK H. MEYER, BECAME INVOLVED IN THE ARTS AND CRAFTS MOVEMENT
AS A YOUNG WOOD CRAFTSMAN IN GERMANY. WITH THE INTENTION OF MAKING ART HIS CAREER, HE
MOVED TO SAN FRANCISCO, OPENED A CABINET SHOP, AND BEGAN TEACHING AT THE MARK HOP-
KINS INSTITUTE OF ART AND THE UNIVERSITY OF CALIFORNIA AT BERKELEY. THE 1906 EARTHQUAKE
LEVELED BOTH HIS SHOP AND THE INSTITUTE. SPEAKING AT AN ARTS AND CRAFTS SOCIETY MEET-

INNO
VATE

C CA C

THIS BROCHURE WAS DESIGNED TO SOLICIT FUNDS FOR THE NEW

CALIFORNIA COLLEGE OF ARTS & CRAFTS
ARCHITECTURE AND DESIGN CAMPUS

THE AUDIENCE FOR THIS PIECE WAS WELL-HEELED DONORS TO THE ARTS. THE FEEL
OF THE BROCHURE HAD TO BE "CONSERVATIVELY PROGRESSIVE" — PROGRESSIVE ENOUGH
FOR A COLLEGE OF ART, BUT CONSERVATIVE ENOUGH FOR AN AUDIENCE UNUSED TO THE
EXPERIMENTAL NATURE OF CONTEMPORARY GRAPHIC DESIGN.

Dum sinunt fata, vivite læti ! *

Seid fröhlich, sooft euch die Möglichkeit geboten
wird und sooft ihr in euch die Kraft findet, denn
Augenblicke reiner Freude bedeuten in unserem
Leben mehr als ganze Tage und Monate, die
wir im trüben Spiel unserer kleinen und großen
Leidenschaften und Begehrlichkeiten verbringen.
(Ihr Drängen ist launisch und ungesund, ihre
Befriedigung ungewiß und von kurzer Dauer,
alles ist Selbstzweck.) Ein Augenblick reiner
Freude bleibt immer in uns, als Glanz, der
niemals verblassen kann.

* Solange es das Schicksal zuläßt: lebt fröhlich !

Vino proleća, praznik je za srce
po kome već jutrom padala je slana,
za srce kom su se otvorile oči
što u prošlost stoje vazdan okrenute,
kad rujnim cvetom procveta obmana,
kad vidik opet oko njega plane
ka onome ko je još na visu,
kad puknu pred njim puteva bele vreže,
kad otvore se u klancu poljane,
a srcem svojim sav život poveže
kao duga planinske daleke strane.
Vino proleća, čudno je za onog
kom svetluca u srcu misao seda,
i bol u sećanju kome oštro seva,
ko počinje s tugom da pripoveda
zamišljen ko utihnula brana,
da se radostima prvih ptica poda,
u šiblje misli rumenih da zaraste
kao u vrbe mlada nadošla voda.

LASZLO MOHOLY – NAGY

Photogrammes
du 8 novembre 1995
au 1er janvier 1996

PICASSO AFRIQUE

Etat d'esprit
du 8 novembre 1995
au 8 janvier 1996

JEAN WIDMER

Graphiste
du 8 novembre 1995
au 12 février 1996

Centre
Georges Pompidou

Press kit and exhibition poster for the center for industrial design at the Centre Georges Pompidou.
Design: Jean Widmer visuel design

THE

(WANG XU)

POSTER

is one of the series posters I was invited to design for the Taiwan Image Poster Design Association, the theme is "Chinese Character".

The simple,clear image of the poster is quite familiar to anyone. But, the stong idea is hidden behind the image. It reflects pictograph as a part of the origin from which the Chinese character has developed, and the splendid Chinese culture in the past. Thus the strength of the culture could be embodied through the clean image. It is the poster I like mostly in this series design.

THE

POSTER

was designed by Ahn Sang-Soo, a graphic designer from Korea.This work possesses the characteristic of Asia design - using bilingual character and expressing the local culture with international visual language to which I share with deep feeling.

This poster reflects the theme of international art festival through type design. You will know the designer's background once you see the work. By using a kind of character drawn with a special pen made by bamboo or leather materials, the way from China, Ahn designed the background to embody dancing abstractly. The music note is symbolized by the logo image and type of "Laughing Stone".

BAUER BODONI

ABCDEFGHIJKLMNOPQRSTUVWXYZ

abcdefghijklmnopqrstuvwxyz

BODONI

ABCDEFGHIJKLMNOPQRSTUVWXYZ
abcdefghijklmnopqrstuvwxyz

FRUTIGER BOLD

ABCDEFGHIJKLMNOPQRSTUVWXYZ
abcdefghijklmnopqrstuvwxyz

HUD BOOK

ABCDEFGHIJKLMNOPQRSTUVWXYZ
abcdefghijklmnopqrstuvwxyz

KAATSKILL BOLD

ABCDEFGHIJKLMNOPQRSTUVWXYZ
abcdefghijklmnopqrstuvwxyz

FUTURA

ABCDEFGHIJKLMNOPQRSTUVWXYZ
abcdefghijklmnopqrstuvwxyz

META NORMAL

ABCDEFGHIJKLMNOPQRSTUVWXYZ
abcdefghijklmnopqrstuvwxyz

FRANKLIN GOTHIC

ABCDEFGHIJKLMNOPQRSTUVWXYZ
abcdefghijklmnopqrstuvwxyz

PRAXIS

ABCDEFGHIJKLMNOPQRSTUVWXYZ
abcdefghijklmnopqrstuvwxyz

RAW BOOK

ABCDEFGHIJKLMNOPQRSTUVWXYZ
abcdefghijklmnopqrstuvwxyz

GROTESQUE MT

ABCDEFGHIJKLMNOPQRSTUVWXYZ
abcdefghijklmnopqrstuvwxyz

SWIFT

ABCDEFGHIJKLMNOPQRSTUVWXYZ
abcdefghijklmnopqrstuvwxyz

GARAMOND

ABCDEFGHIJKLMNOPQRSTUVWXYZ
abcdefghijklmnopqrstuvwxyz

ADOBE GARAMOND

ABCDEFGHIJKLMNOPQRSTUVWXYZ
abcdefghijklmnopqrstuvwxyz

TRIXIE TEXT

ABCDEFGHIJKLMNOPQRSTUVWXYZ
abcdefghijklmnopqrstuvwxyz

GILL SANS

ABCDEFGHIJKLMNOPQRSTUVWXYZ
abcdefghijklmnopqrstuvwxyz

CHARLES S. ANDERSON *(PGS. 92-93) FAVORITE TYPEFACES: Todder Stencil, 20th Century Metal Cut Version, Plastic Menu, Garamond Metal Cut Version, Venus Bold Metal Cut Version*

PHIL BAINES *(PGS. 94-95) My five favorite typefaces keep changing, but are generally the five I'm using at any given moment; right now they are Amerigo, Argo, Strayhorn, Sohia, Swift.*

BEN BOS *(PGS. 98-99) FAVORITE TYPEFACES: Akzidenz Grotesk Medium, Serifa Medium, (linotype) Centennial 55, (Enschedé) Trinité 3 condensed semi-bold, (Berthold) Bodoni regular/semi-bold*

LAURIE DEMARTINO *(PGS. 110-111) FAVORITE TYPEFACES: News Gothic, New Baskerville, Futura Book lowercase (with just the right amount of letterspacing), Dictionary Type, Trajan*

ALAN FLETCHER *(PGS. 120-121) (Left) I don't really have a piece of favorite typography that I have done over the last three years. At the moment I feel quite warm about this anagram I constructed out of a design produced by somebody else—whoever it is (or was) that did the typography on cartons used by Evian, the producers of a French mineral water. (Right) I like this piece of work, designed and printed by Alan Kitching, because it relies on exploiting a fixed set of ingredients. It also manages to convey a sense of craft as well as technology, of tradition as well as innovation, of rawness and elegance. That's not an inconsiderable achievement. FAVORITE TYPEFACES: Baskerville, Gill, Firmin Didot, Sans Serif Shaded, Thorowgood Italic*

MARK GEER *(PGS. 126-127) FAVORITE TYPEFACES: Adobe Garamond, Bauer Bodoni, Centaur, Futura, Univers*

KAN TAI-KEUNG *(PGS. 136-137) (Left page, top and bottom) A set of four posters specially designed for an invitation show. Chinese calligraphy and traditional writing tools reflect the sentimental ties between designers and Chinese characters.(Center) A poster to promote an art exhibition in Los Angeles. In it, "L" is two simple black bars while the small letter "a" is composed of a jade ring and a Chinese ink brushstroke. The idea of putting together the things from East and West was inspired by the nature of the show. The color strips and blue background is an idea taken from the US flag and represents the venue of the exhibition.(Right page) TEE magazine invited several internationally famous designers to view the developmental trend of typography in the 21st century from various ethical perspectives. "T" is presented by a Chinese ink brush stroke and an inking stick, together with geometrical forms of "Y", "P" and "O"as the structure to show the new vision of oriental culture in typographic design. FAVORITE TYPEFACES: Bodoni, Garamond, Futura, Univers, Avant Garde*

KOEWEIDEN POSTMA ASSOCIATES *(PG. 144) One poster out of a series of five which feature Scotty Pippen, Andre Agassi, Michael Johnson, Jason Kid and Monica Seles. We've chosen this series because we like it the most at this moment. (Pg. 145, top) This piece of Toon Michiels is our favorite because of the personal and emotional statements which are integrated in a beautiful and daring way. (Pg. 145, bottom) Xmas, Boxrel, 1954, St. Oedenrode. 1996. Illustration from the Take 2 calendar/1997 by Toon Michiels. FAVORITE TYPEFACES: 1. All the Saul Bass title-scores for the films of Martin Scorcese 2. Type as handled by Peter Saville*

ITALO LUPI *(PGS. 152-153) (Top left) April 1997 page of Grafiche Mariano calendar.The selection of this work comes from the great love I have for "Lettera 1" type. This love was born in 1959 when, as a young boy, I bought that basic book "Lettera" by Armin Haab and Alex Socker, that published this type sans-serif, black, very strong with such perfect proportions and adaptations. In this sheet of the calendar I have "ill-treated" it with the help of a computer, in a game of forced perspectives. (Pg. 153) The well-known poster for IBM drawn by Paul Rand (practically without typography) in 1981 (with the eye, the bee and the M on black background) is a project which has particularly influenced me: it helped everybody understand that you could go beyond the letters with a substitute metaphor, something first explored by Gene Federico, then by Lubalin and, in a misleading way, also by Franco Grignani. FAVORITE TYPEFACES: Bodoni Light, Futura Bold, OCR-B (capital only), News Gothic, Torino Corsivo*

MICHAEL MABRY *(PGS. 154-155) FAVORITE TYPEFACES: News Gothic, Bauer Bodoni, Bembo, Franklin, Typewriter*

PIERRE MENDELL *(PGS. 160-161) FAVORITE TYPEFACES: Univers, Bodoni, Frutiger, Futura, Franklin Gothic*

TOON MICHIELS *(PG. 162) "Ik wil spielen" or "I WANT TO PLAY" is a strong guideline for every typographer, yound or old. For me typography is (in origin) about handwriting. (PG. 163) "MIND THE GAP" is another strong guideline for all of us. I like the idea of comparing soccer with design, in particular between England and the Netherlands, and to be honest the English play a better game most of the time. Thank you Jacques and Paul (Koeweiden Postma associates) for your strong creative reminder. FAVORITE TYPEFACES: Bodoni, Garamond, Joanna, Gill, News Gothic*

PATRICK MITCHELL *(PGS. 164-165) FAVORITE TYPEFACES: Monotype Grotesque, Bell Gothic, Kaatskill, News Gothic, Trade Gothic*

ROGER PFUND (PG. 178) Photograph of a Greek typographic blackboard, Greece, photo by Roger Pfund. More than explanation, this typographic subject inspires statements like: 'Typographic innocence,' 'Primitive calligraphy,' 'Spontaneity,' 'Art of accident,' 'Mixture of culture,' 'Without any correction,' 'Without failure,' 'Rigorous.' (Pg. 179) Label for wine spirit Williamine, offset printing on Japanese paper. In my work, typography often not only conveys a message, but also reinforces the image, or better yet, is itself the image.

WOODY PIRTLE (PGS. 180-181) My typographic repertoire includes, of course, all the traditional components: headlines, text, captions, pull quotes, drop caps, etc., but my typographic performance is definitely at its most compelling level when I am creating my own letter forms or manipulating existing ones for use in symbols and/or logotypes. What I look for is a commonality or juxtaposition of form that makes the letters become an inextricable part of an overall design. This creates a sense of inevitability in the solution, as evidenced in these symbols/logotypes for En Garde Arts, a New York-based Off-Broadway theater company, and En Garde Events, a company that produces media events. FAVORITE TYPEFACES: Bauer Bodoni, Bembo, Caslon 540, Didot, Garamond #3, Times Roman, Trajan, Alternate Gothic, Franklin Gothic, Futura, Gill Sans, Liteline Gothic

LEX REITSMA (PGS. 184-185) In 1990 I was asked by the newly-appointed artistic director Pierre Audi to develop a new graphic style for the Dutch National Opera. From that moment on, I designed all posters and programs as well as the typographic logo that is still being used. I have chosen to relate the posters to the atmosphere and period style of the stage productions. Initially this led to typographic posters in which pictures were used as a second, underlying layer. Recent posters are more photograph oriented, and use photographs that are sometimes manipulated by computer. The typography is nearly always clear. Communication is the first priority. My work is inspired by the found or self-produced images that relate to the subject matter of the design. These form the starting point for all my typographic activity.

LANA RIGSBY (PGS. 186-187) Design and the Bottom Line: I've always enjoyed the idea that type can be used as a "picture" rather than as characters to be read. For "Design and the Bottom Line" we directly lifted a screen display of stock quotes; and by repeating, distorting, and reversing it, made an inference about the way information is disseminated. GENERAL THOUGHTS ON TYPOGRAPHY: As a kid I was lectured that profanity–"talking trash"–was the sure sign of an underdeveloped vocabulary and a too-small grasp of the English language. Gradually I've come to understand that the opposite is true. Direct talk requires a nuanced mastery that sometimes goes beyond any sense of the beautiful or correct. So it is with type. It takes guts and eloquence to use the bad stuff to do what the good stuff can't. That, and a willingness to say what you really mean.

SAMPLES I LIKE OR HAVE BEEN INSPIRED BY:"Manga," Japan's ubiquitious adult street comics blur the line between words and pictures. They're "read" in a layered rather than linear order; letters and works are part of the image as opposed to being confined to text balloons. Manga has a visual vocabulary for almost every sound effect, including the sound of silence (SHIIIIN). Osamu Tezuka predicted that Manga would become "the language of the space age."Typographically, I think it's a natural progression in the evolutionary merging of words, pictures, and ideas. FAVORITE TYPEFACES: Thesis, Garamond, Helvetica Neue, Goudy, Sabon

STEVE SANDSTROM (PGS. 188-189) FAVORITE TYPEFACES: Century Schoolbook, Garamond No. 3, Din, Franklin Gothic

PAULA SCHER (PGS. 190-191) Generally I work with typography to accomplish two goals: 1) to convey information; 2) to convey spirit, mood, personality, and ideas. I often use type as image, as these two posters illustrate. "Art is..." is the verbal slogan assigned by Silas Rhodes for an anniversary poster for the School of Visual Arts. The words are filled with a handwritten listing of all my favorite artists and form the typeface "Grotesque." In the subway, the poster becomes interactive.

MICHAEL VANDERBYL (PGS 200-201) A piece of inspiration (not pictured): "Pastee," by John Bielenberg. FAVORITE TYPEFACES: Garamond Expert, OCR-B, Trajan.

JOVICA VELJOVIC (PGS. 202-203) The reasons why I am choosing these two works are typographical clarity and simplicity. I also wanted to show that writing is still an important part of language and therefore of typography. I am tired of confetti typography! I also know that I am now in the minority, but it's fine with me. FAVORITE TYPEFACES: Diotima (letterpress) by Gudrum Zapfvon Hesse, Trinité by Bram de Does, Optima by Hermann Zapf, Avenir by Adrian Frutiger, Mantinia by Matthew Carter

JEAN WIDMER (PGS. 204-205) This poster presented various problems, as it had to announce three different exhibitions of three artists from three generations. The exhibitions were staged in spaces on three floors of the Centre Pompidou. I opted for graphic design and typography inspired by the beginnings of the Bauhaus in the 1930s. The drawn letters allowed for some ligatures, creating a certain rhythm in the order and design of the page.

WANG XU (PGS. 206-207) FAVORITE TYPEFACES: Univers, Avenir, Syntax, Myria, Frutiger

AA - Author's Alteration, which covers any line or art changes made after a document has been set; any change other than a Printers' Error (PE).

ACUTE - accents placed above a letter, for example: á é ó, etc. In romanized Chinese, these marks indicate a rise in tone.

ADNATE - to flow evenly from the stem of a letter as opposed to abrupt.

AESC - (pronounced ash, originally written as aesc) ae is a common ligature of Greek origin taken from ai (alpha iota) still existing in alglosaxon, Danish and Norwegian alphabets. In Swedish, it has been reduced to ä.

AGATE - a unit of measurement used in newspapers to determine column depth/size. One inch is equal to 14 agate lines.

ALDINE - any typography resembling the publishing house of Aldus Manitus, which he ran in Venice during the years 1494-1515. Also any type resembling those designed by Francesco Griffo.

ALIGNMENT - arranging letters along a line so the bases of each character all rest on a line with only the descenders hanging below (also called base aligning). Arranging characters across a line so they appear even on both sides, or they are even on the right side and ragged on the left, or even on the left and ragged on the right or with an equal number of characters on either side of the center of the line with ragged left and right sides (see also centered, flush, FL, FR, justified and ragged).

ANALPHABETIC - not alphabetic, a character such as an umlaut, acute, accent, asterisk and dagger, used with the alphabet, but lacking a correct place in the alphabetic order.

APERTURE - the opening in such lowercase letters as c,e,s, a and uppercase letters like C and S.

APEX - the outside part of a character where two lines meet, such as the points of an A,M,N, etc.

APOSTROPHE - originally used to serve as indication of exclusion of letters, it hass grown to include a representation of the possessive. It is also called a raised comma or single close quote. When used alone, it indicates a glottal stop and in Slavic and Native American languages, it indicates a modified pronunciation of consonants.

ARM - any stroke of a letter that reaches up diagonally or horizontally across the top and is not contained within the letter, as in the upper branches of a y or the cross of a t.

ARABIC NUMERALS - characters named for their origination in Arabia. The numerals 0-9 and any combinations thereof which are commonly used today, as opposed to roman numerals.

ASCENDER - the portion of a lowercase letter that rises above the x-height/mean line/body of a letter.

ASTERISK - a character that has been in use for over 5,000 years with origins dating back to ancient Sumerian pictographs. It is used to mark references, keywords, missing letters or words, or to mark the year of birth.

ASYMMETRICAL - a type of alignment in typography whereby neither the left nor the right edges of a column bear any visual relationship to one another.

ATF - American Type Founders, founded in 1892 by acquiring a number of smaller organizations. It has become the largest type foundry in North America.

AXIS - refers to the angle of the stroke, which points to the angle of the implement used to draw the letter.

BACKSLANT - a typeface that slants to the left (the opposite direction of italic). Used primarily for special effect.

BACKSLASH - a product of the computer age with no valid function in tyography.

BALL TERMINAL - a ball-like form at the terminus of an arm in such letters as a, c, j and y.

BASELINE - the imaginary line on which letters rest, below which descenders extend (see also top line, mid-line and beardline).

BASTARDA - one of the five major families in the blackletter types.

BAR - a horizontal line that is integrated into the form of the letters H, T. Also used in mathematics to symbolize absolute value.

BARRED H - one of the ISO characters omitted from most fonts, it comes from th Maltese alphabet.

BARRED L - Routinely included in standard text fonts, this letter is from the Polish and several Native American alphabets.

BARRED O - also known as an O-slash, this letter is from the Norwegian and Danish alphabets (similar to the swedish ö).

BARRED T - one of the ISO characters omitted from most fonts, originally from the Lapp alphabet.

BEARDLINE - the line on which the bottom of descenders rest.

BEAK TERMINAL - a harsher version of a ball terminal.

BEZIER CURVES - a critical element in the Postscript language, a series of lines drawn to specific series of coordinates to create a curve.

BICAMERAL - two alphabets joined (such as our alphabet with upper amd lowercase letters).

BITMAP - a series of dots that comprises the visual image of a character. Made up on pixels, it often creates a jagged image.

BLACKLETTER - tall, narrow and pointed letterforms based on medieval script. The five major groups are: Bastarda, Fraktur, Quadrata, Rotunda and Textura.

BLIND FOLIO - a counted page with no visible page number.

BLUEPRINTS - photoprints of blue ink on blue paper, used as a preliminary proof to check art position and text; also known as blues.

BODY - the unit that carries each typographic character, either a metal block (in traditional foundry type) or an imaginary block surrounding each character (in digital typesetting).

BODY MATTER/BODY COPY - the primary reading material as opposed to pull-quotes, headlines, lead-ins, etc.

BODY SIZE - the height of a typeface, traditionally measured in points, however it is sometimes measured in didot points in European typefaces. This encompasses the entire space allocated to each letter (allowing for appropriate letterspacing) not just the visible dimensions of the letter. Using letterpress terminology, it is the depth of the body of the type. Also known as type size.

BODY TYPE - the type used for the main body of a printed piece, usually between 6-14 points.

BREVE - an accent used in English for vowel pronunciation and in Malay, Rumanian and Turkish on both consonants and vowels.

BROWNPRINT - a copy made from a negative, used as a for-position-only proof before making a printing plate; also known as a brownline or van Dyke.

BULK - measured in pages per inch (PPI), the thickness of papers used for printing.

CAP HEIGHT - the height, from baseline to the top, of a capital letter.

CARET - although a basic symbol used by editors and proofreaders, it is a product of the computer generation and has a very limited use in typography, therefore it is not found among the ISO character set.

CARON - an inverted circumflex found in the Croatian, Czech, Lapp, Lithuanian, Native American and Slovakian languages on both consonants and vowels.

CASTING - a process in setting type during which liquid metal is poured into type molds.

CASTING OFF - calculating the number of lines a manuscript will be when set in a particular typeface and size by dividing the character count of the manuscript by the Characters Per Pica (CPP) figure.

CEDILLA - literally, little z. An accent used with consonants such as the French, Portuguese and Turkish c.

CENTERED - a typographic term describing the alignment when characters are positioned an equal distance originating from the actual center of a page, causing a ragged left and right margin which, on any given line, are the mirror image of one another.

CHANCERY - a group of letterforms distinguished by their long, curved extenders and elegant appearance (see also SWASH).

CHARACTER COUNT - total number of characters and spaces to be typeset, may be by the line, paragraph, page or document.

CHARACTERS - any letter, numeral, punctuation mark, figure, etc.

CHARACTERS PER PICA - (CPP) the average number of characters that will fit into one pica of line space when set in a particular typeface and size.

CICERO - a unit of measurement, predominant in Europe equal to 12 Didot points slightly larger than a pica, it is .178 inch.

CIRCUMFLEX - In French, Portuguese, Rumanian and Welsh, an accent used on vowels.

Cold Type - type created without casting, as in in a typewriter, for example, where the letter is struck onto the page.

Colophon - information contained at the end of a book describing production credits.

Color - the shade (lightness or darkness) of a segment of type. This is affected by the face, point size, leading and tracking.

Column Inch - a measurement used in newspapers that is one column wide and one inch high.

Column Rule - a thin rule used to separate columns.

Column Width - the measurement of a column of type from left to right.

Combs - vertical slashes on horizontal rules. Most commonly seen as guidelines for information one fills in on a form.

Composing Stick - a tray-like accoutrement with adjustable line measures used when hand-setting type.

Composition - assembling characters into words, sentences. manuscripts, etc. by hand, hot metal machine, photosetting or digitally.

Condensed - a more narrow version of a particular typeface.

Contrast - the amount of variance between the thick and thin strokes of a letter.

Corps - European measurement, slightly smaller than a point.

Counter - the white space, either wholly or partially enclosed by the strokes of a letter, such as in a, e, c, m, etc.

CPI - (Characters Per Inch) a measurement of storage space/density of a magnetic tape or disc or any other linear recording device.

CPS - (Characters Per Second) the way the spread of a phototypesetting machine's output is measured.

Cross Bar - the horizontal stroke in such letters as A, H, t, etc.

Crosshead - a title or heading centered above the body text.

Cursive - typefaces that resemble handwriting because of their fluid strokes, connecting letters and curved lines.

Dagger - a symbol used to indicate a footnote. Also used in Europe to indicate the year of demise.

Descender - the part of a lowercase letter that hangs below the baseline.

Dieresis/Umlaut - an accent used with vowels: ä, ë, etc. indicating a separation of adjacent vowels or a change in pronunciation in such languages as French, German, Swedish, Turkish, Portuguese, Spanish, English and Welsh.

Didot - a European measurement roughly equivalent to a point.

Dimension Sign - (multiplication sign) see mathematics symbols.

Dingbat - an ornamental character used to attract attention.

Display Type - generally intended to attract attention, this type is set apart from the body, usually 18 points or larger. See also headline type.

Dot Leader - a series of dots intended to guide a reader's eye from one point to another, as in a table of contents.

Double Acute - a Hungarian accent (often called a Hungarian Umlaut) used with o and u.

Double Bar - a traditional reference and bibliographic mark.

Double Dagger - used for footnotes, also called a double obelisk.

Double Prime - abbreviation for seconds of arc or, more commonly, inches.

DPI - (Dots Per Inch) a measurement of resolution, used in reference to typography and laser output devices. The lower the DPI, the more jagged an object appears, the higher the DPI, the more solid and fluid it appears.

Drop Cap - (drop intial) a display character set at the beginning of a line that falls far below the baseline, generally to the baseline of one of the following lines.

Drop Folio - a page number that is positioned on the bottom of a page, when the balance of the page numbers appear on the top of the page. Traditionally, this occurs on the first page of a chapter.

Drop paragraph/Dropline paragraph - a paragraph that begins immediately after the period of the preceding paragraph, with only a line separating them.

Dry Transfer - a process of rubbing type from a sheet of lettering onto a receptive surface, thereby eliminating some setting.

Dyet - a Croatian letter.

Ear - a decorative but unnecessary stroke attached to the bowl of a g or the stem of an r.

Elevated Cap - an initial capital letter set in a larger point size than the body, but resting on the same baseline as the balance of the type of that line.

Elite - smallest size of traditional typewriter type, with 12 characters per inch (see also pica).

Ellipsis - three dots indicating an omission.

EM - a measure of linear space equal to the point size of the typeface, therefore, in 10pt. type, an em is 10 pts. Based on the letter m, which is usually the same width as the type size. Typically used to measure the width of a column or size of an indent.

EM Dash - a dash one em long.

EM-Quad - (mutton) a space character that is the square of the type size, so for a 12 pt. type, it would be 12 pts. high by 12 pts. wide, roughly one EM squared.

EN - a measure of linear space that is one half the point size of a typeface, so in a twelve point typeface, an en is 6 pts. or one half of EM. Based on the letter n, which is usually one half the width of the type size.

EN-Dash - a dash the length of an EN. Often used to replace the words to or through as in 1-10.

ENG - one of the ISO characters from the Lapp alphabet. The lowercase symbol is commonly used in linguistics to represent the sound made by the ng combination.

Enlarger Font - a font made from negative film used for point sizes larger than 16 or 18 points.

EN-Quad - (nut) a space character that is one half of the type size squared, so with a 12 pt. type, an en quad would be 6 pts. high by 6 pts. wide, roughly one EN squared.

Eszett - (sharp s) a ligature for ss, used when setting German.

Eth - a letter from the Icelandic and Old English alphabets. Although representing a different sound, the uppercase Eth looks the same as the uppercase Dyet.

Ethel - a French ligature also seen in archaic English, corresponding to the Greek omicron iota. It can be found in words borrowed from the Greek, like Oedipus.

Extenders - strokes of a letter that cause it to pass below the baseline or above the mid-line (see ascenders and decenders)

Extended/Expanded - stretching a typeface beyond its normal width.

Eye - see Bowl. An open eye is an aperture and a large eye refers to the x-height.

Family - all sizes, styles and other variations of a typeface.

FL - (flush left) alignment so that the left side is even and the right side jagged.

FL&R - (flush left and right, also known as justified) a typographic alignment so that both sides are even.

Flueron - flower or leaf-like dingbat used for decorative purposes.

Flush and Hung - Alignment whereby the first line is flush left, while the balance of the paragraph is indented. Commonly used in glossaries and indices (see also hanging indent).

Folio - page number.

Font - the total set of all characters in a particular typeface and size.

Font Driver - a computer file that determines what character shall be defined by a particular code.

Foot Margin - the white space at the bottom of the page.

Fore-Edge - the outside margin of a page (opposite the binding only).

Founders'/ Foundry type - metal characters used in hand setting type.

Foundry - place where type is manufactured.

FR - (flush right) alignment whereby the right side of the line all rests evenly on the margin and the left side is ragged.

Fraktur - one of the five families of blackletter type.

Gallery Proof - (rough proof) a rough presentation of a document to judge if it has been set properly.

Glottal Stop - actually a sound as opposed to a letter. Represented by an apostrophe as in Qur'an.

Grave - an accent used with vowels in such languages as French, Italian and msny others.

Guillements - (chevron) single and double quotation marks used in Europe, Asia and Africa.

Grosteque - another name for sans serif typefaces.

Gutter - the empty space between columns of text, also the space between two facing pages, allowing additional room for binding.

Hairline rule - the finest line an output device is capable of producing; usually 1/4 pt. rule.

Half-Tone - pieces of film converted from images into camera-ready form, with an increased or descreased number of dots causing the variations between light and dark areas.

Hanging Indent - typographic alignment in which the first line is set to the left margin and the balance of the paragraph is indented (see also flush and hung).

Hanging Initial - a letter placed in the left margin.

Hanging Punctuation - punctuation marks set past the literal margin in order to achieve the appearance of being flush with the margin.

Head Margin - white space on the top of the page.

Hint - guides used by a computer to accurately fill in the space allotted to each letter.

Hot Type - the process of casting type from hot metal in order to print.

Humanist - letterforms more akin to human handwriting. There are two kinds: Roman fonts based on Carolingian script and italics.

Humanist Axis - an oblique stroke axis reflecting the natural slants of human handwriting.

Impose - composing/marking up the pages for reproduction.

Imposition - arranging pages so that when they are printed, folded and trimmed, they will be in the right order.

Incunabula - 15th century printing.

Inferior characters - small characters positioned at or below the baseline.

Inline - when the strokes of a letter are carved out, leaving a white area.

Inverted Comma - see quotation marks.

ISO - International Organization for Standardization - an international organization striving for industrial and scientific standards.

Italic - a broad term for a version of a typeface that slants to the right, generally credited with having evolved from chancery script.

ITC - International Typeface Corporation. New York based typeface distributing and licensing corporation founded in 1970.

Justify/Justified Type - when a line of type is both flush left and flush right.

Kern - causing the letters to be closer together than is standard. (see also letterspacing and tracking).

Lachrymal Terminal - see teardrop terminal.

Leads - (pronounced leds) when typesetting by hand, metal bars placed above and below lines of text to modify line spacing.

Leaders - a series of dots, dashes etc., meant to guide the reader's eye across the page, as in a table of contents.

Leading/Ledding - the amount of space between lines of text (see also leads).

Lead-In - the beginning few words of copy that is set apart from the body by using bold, italic or all caps.

Leg - downward angled stroke of such letters as k and r.

Letter Fit - the quality of letterspacing.

Letter Spacing - modifying the traditional amount of space between letters (see also kerning and tracking).

Ligature - joining of two or more letters as in æ.

Lightface - a variation of the blackness of a typeface.

Line Spacing - see leading.

Lining Figures - numerals whose height is equivalent to that of the capital letters in a particular typeface.

Link - the stroke that connects the bowl and the loop of letters such as the lowercase g.

Linotype - a method of setting type a line at a time (see also monotype).

Loop - the rounded stroke that is not a literal part of the character, such as the bottom embellishment of the lowercase g.

Lowercase Figures - the smaller letters of a font, also called miniscules.

Lowline - a baseline rule, identical with an underscore.

M/3 - one-third of an EM.

Macron - a horizontal line appearing over a vowel indicating a modifi-

cation in pronounciation.

Master Proof - a version of a document reflecting all corrections to be made (a combination of the PE's and AA's).

Matrix - in metal typesetting, the mold from which type is cast.

Mean line - the line that rests on the top of the lowercase letters (without ascenders).

Mid Space - a space that is one-fourth of an EM.

Miniscules - the lowercase letters of a font.

Minus Leading - setting type so that the space between baseline and baseline is less than the height of the type itself, thereby allowing ascenders and descenders to overlap.

Minus Letterspacing - reducing the space between letters to a level below normal (see kerning).

Modern figures - see lining figures.

Modulation - the variation in the width of the strokes of a letterform based upon the appearance of the letters as they were once written with a broad nub pen.

Monospace - setting type so that each character occupies an equal amount of line space, such as is done on a typewriter.

Monotype - setting type a character at a time (see also linotype).

Mu - Greek lowercase m, also the prefix for micro.

Mutton - see EM Quad.

Oblique - typefaces with an angled axis such as italics.

Obelisk - see dagger.

OCR - (optical character recognition) devices that can scan a document, reading the type, and allow it to be processed by a computer.

Octothorp - the number sign (#).

Ognek - in Navajo, Polish and Lithuanian, an accent used with vowels.

Old Style Figures - numbers that have ascenders and descenders and vary in size.

Optical Alignment/Optical Volumes - modifying letters' positions so that they appear to be correctly aligned.

Orphan - a single word at the top of a page, left over from the preceding paragraph (see also widow).

Overdot - in Polish, an accent used with consonants and in Lithuanian and Turkish, used with vowels.

Overscore - a line set above type.

Pantograph - an instrument capable of transferring a design by tracing the master drawing.

PE - abbreviation for printer's error. This term covers any sort of error made by the typesetter as opposed to the author or the editor.

Phototypesetting - setting type using a keyboard for input and a photo unit for the output.

PI Characters - special characters such as mathematical symbols and reference marks that are not normally in a particular typeface.

Pica - 12 points or 1/6 of an inch. Also refers to 12 point type, one of the two sizes found on typewriters (see also elite).

Piece Fraction - a fraction that does not exist in a character set and must be composed with two numbers and a solidus.

Pilcrow - another word for the paragraph symbol.

Point - a typographic unit of measurement, equivalent to .0138" or .351 mm in the US and .346 mm in Europe.

Point Size - the size of a particular typeface measured from the top of the ascenders to the bottom of the descenders.

Posture - the angle of the typeface, Roman is vertical and italic is oblique, etc.

Prime - an abbreviation for feet and minutes of arc.

Punch - metal bar containing the master design of a type character.

Punchcutter - a skilled craftsman who sets type designs directly into the metal bars of the punch.

Quad - in metal typesetting, a piece that is less than type-high with no purpose other than to generate white space, thereby filling out lines of type.

Quotation Marks - also known as inverted commas.

Ragged - setting lines of type so that either the left or the right side is jagged (see FL and FR).

Raised Comma - see apostrophe, glottal stop, and quotation marks.

Recto - right hand page of a bound document, always bearing an odd number (opposite of verso).

Register Marks - marks placed on document to aid in correct positioning.

Reversed Out - white type on black or other dark background.

Reverse Video - digitally set white type on dark background.

Ranging Figures - figures of even height (see lining figures).

Raster - digital grid (see hint).

Rationalist Axis - vertical axis, as in Roman type.

Roman - type with vertical axis.

Rotunda - a class of Blackletter types.

Rough Rag - flush left type set with no hyphenations, allowing for strongly contrasting line lengths.

Rule - a typographic line.

Runaround - setting type around an image so that the type reflects the shape of the graphic.

Sans Serif - any of several letterforms consisting of single simple uniform strokes without embellishment. This term is used as a classification for all typefaces containing these letterforms.

Scaling Font - a digital font whose weight and proportions vary according to the size in which it is set.

Script - a style of typeface designed to resemble handwriting, script typefaces contain very slight thick and thin stroke contrasts; the letters flow together, are connecting and are usually on an incline. This term is also used as a classification for all typefaces containing these letterforms.

Section - the double s used in legal writing.

Serif - small horizontal embellishments appearing at the end of the main strokes of letterforms. This term is used as a classification for all typefaces containing these letterforms.

Sidehead - a title or subhead set flush left or slightly indented.

Slab Serif - an abrupt serif in the same thickness as the main stroke.

Slope - angle of inclination of the stems and extenders.

Small Caps - capital letters that appear the same size as the x-height of lowercase letters.

Solid - setting type where the leading is equal to the point size.

Solidus - the line dividing the numerator and denominator in a fraction.

Stem - the main stroke of a letter, not part of a bowl.

Stempel - a German foundry in existence from 1895-1985.

Stress - direction of thickening in a curved stroke.

Stroke - principal line of a character.

Subhead - secondary headline set smaller than the headline, but apart from the body copy.

Subscript - a character that prints below the baseline.

Superscript - a character that prints above the mean-line.

Swash - letterforms that are overly decorative (usually script or Italic typefaces).

Tail - the slanted line in the R, K, and Q.

Teardrop Terminal - a swelling at the end of the arm in letters like f, g, j, y etc.

Terminal - the end of a letter stroke when it is not a serif.

Text Block - the part of the page occupied by text.

Text Figures - numeric figures designed to match the lowercase letters of a particular face in both size and color.

Textura - a class of Blackletter type.

Text Letters - a style of typeface that was designed to resemble the handdrawn letterforms of scribes and calligraphers. This term is used as a classification for all typefaces containing these letterforms.

Text Type - see body type.

Texture - determined by posture, size, weight, leading and structure of an area of type.

Thick space - a space measuring one-third of an EM.

Thin space - a space measuring between one fifth or one sixth of an EM.

Three-To-Em - one third EM; also written M/3.

Tight Rag - FL type set using hyphens, so the edges have a less severe rag.

Tilde - in Spanish and Philipino, a symbol combined with consonants and used with vowels in Portuguese.

Titling Figures - numeric figures designed to match the uppercase letters of a typeface in size and color.

Tracking - modifying letter and word spacing to make text fit in a certain amount of space.

Transfer Type - type that is set by rubbing letters from a sheet onto a mechanical or other receptive surface.

Transitive - serif that flows from the main stroke without reversing direction. Common amongst italic and script letterforms.

Tricameral - an alphabet with three cases, such as uppercase, lowercase, and small caps.

Turnovers - second and subsequent lines of bulleted items indented an equal distance as the first line from the bullet.

Typeface - a named type design, as in Times Roman, Garamond, etc.

Type Family - all existing variations of a typeface (Roman, Italic, bold, condensed, expanded, etc.)

Type Measurement - type is measured vertically in points (1/72", the larger the point size, the larger the letter) and horizontally in picas (1/16", the larger the pica size, the longer the line).

Typographer - despite various connotations this word has adopted, it simply means one who sets type.

Typography - the art of working with and designing type.

U/lc - an abbreviaton for the typesetting direction upper and lower case.

Underdot - An accent used with consonants in Asian, Arabic, Hebrew, African and Native American languages.

Unicameral - alphabets having only one case, such as Arabic and Hebrew.

Umlaut - see Dieresis.

Variable Space - when each letter is afforded a different amount of space based on its shape.

Versal - a large initial cap, either elevated or dropped.

Verso - the right hand (even numbered) page of a document (see RECTO).

Vertical Rule - see Bar.

Weight - the darkness of a typeface.

Whiteletter - light Roman and italic typefaces popular with 19th century Humanists.

White Line - a line space.

Widow - a single word that carries into the following column or page (see orphan).

Word Spacing - the amount of space between each word which, although different because of the different characters, is adjusted with optical alignment to make it appear to be equal spacing. The words must not be too close together to be difficult to read, nor too distant to look like separate units. One suggestion to provide moderate word spacing is to visualize the letter n without letterspacing between each word; to achieve a tighter word spacing, picture the letter i with letterspacing between each word.

WYSIWYG - What You See Is What You Get, a term referring to the appearance of a document on a computer monitor when it is pictured exactly as it will appear when output.

X-Height - the height of lowercase letters from the baseline to the x-line.

X-Line - see mean line.

CHARLES S. ANDERSON

Charles S. Anderson is founder of the design firm of the same name. Founded in 1989, Charles S. Anderson Design Company specializes in product design and development, consulting, naming, identity, and package design. The firm has worked with clients such as The French Paper Company, Polo Ralph Lauren, Nike, Levi's, *The New York Times*, Nissan, Urban Outfitters, Fossil, Sierra Designs, and Sony.

PHIL BAINES

Phil Baines lives and works in London. He has been a freelance graphic designer since 1987, mainly for art galleries and publishers but he also does some animated typographic sequences for TV commercials. Since September 1991 he's been a senior lecturer in graphic design at Central Saint Martins College of Art and Design. His two typefaces for *Fuse* are CanYou? and Ushaw.

DEREK BIRDSALL

Derek Birdsall has worked as a freelance graphic designer from his studio in Covent Garden (later Islington) since 1961. He was a founding partner, in 1983, of the Omnific Studios Partnership; a consultant designer for the *The Independent* magazine from 1989 to 1993; tutor and designer of the house-style for Prince of Wales's Institute of Architecture in 1991; and since 1992 has been design consultant for the National Art Collections Fund. Birdsall has broadcast on TV and radio on design subjects and his catalogue designs for major museums throughout the world have won many awards, including the 1987 New York Art Directors' Club Gold Medal for "Shaker Design."

BEN BOS

From 1954 to 1962 Ben Bos was a copywriter, then later a designer and art director with Ahrend, a Dutch office furniture and equipment firm. He then joined the first Dutch multi-disciplinary design group, Total Design. In 1966 he was appointed Creative Director; he left in 1991. Presently an independent designer and consultant, Bos is responsible for such corporate identities as Randstad staffing services, Generale Bank (Belgium), Furness Group, Middle East Bank, and City of Capelle.

PIERLUIGI CERRI

Pierluigi Cerri is one of the founders of Gregotti Associati. He is a member of the *Alliance Graphique Internationale*. He was art director of the Biennale of Venice in 1976 and of Electa Editrice publishing house. He is editor of *Casabella* and *Rassegna* magazines and is responsible for the graphic image of Palazzo Grassi in Venice and of the *Kunst- und Ausstellunghalle der Bundesrepublik Deutschland* in Bonn. He is art director of the interactive series Encyclomedia (books on CD-ROM), directed by Umberto Eco; he has developed the visual identity of many events, including Italia 90 World Soccer Championship, and is an image consultant for Unifor, Ferrari Auto Lingotto.

ALAN COLVIN

In 1982, Alan Colvin graduated from Texas Tech University. After working for a year in Houston, he returned to his hometown of Dallas to work for Woody Pirtle, where he produced work for clients including TGI Friday's, Boy Scouts of America, and Neocon. In 1988, Colvin formed a partnership with Joe Rattan. Colvin Rattan Design specialized in corporate identity and collateral design. Clients included Apple Computer, National Gypsum Co, and Word Publishing. In 1991, Alan moved to the west coast to work as a lead designer for Nike. In 1994, Alan joined Joe Duffy Design. While at Duffy, he has worked on projects for Black & Decker, Jim Beam Brands, Stroh Brewery, and Nikon.

LAURIE DeMARTINO

Laurie DeMartino began her career in New York working with a design studio which focused primarily on packaging for corporate cosmetic clients such as Prescriptives, Estee Lauder, Elizabeth Arden, and Lancome. She then ran her own independent design studio in Philadelphia. She has developed logos, identity programs, packaging, book design, and literature for a broad range of clients from international corporations to non-profit organizations. Some of Laurie's clients include Earle Palmer Brown, Campbell Soup Company, Concierge Software Company, Anthropologie, and French Paper Company.

ALAN FLETCHER

Alan Fletcher began his career in New York where he worked for *Fortune* magazine, the Container Corporation, and IBM. He moved back to London and in 1962 co-founded Fletcher/Forbes/Gill, which served such clients as Pirelli, Cunard, Penguin Books, and Olivetti. He co-founded Pentagram in 1972 and created design programmes for Reuters, BP, Lucas Industries, The Mandarin Oriental Hotel Group, Lloyd's of London, Daimler Benz, Arthur Andersen & Co, and ABB. In 1992 he left Pentagram to work alone in his own studio. Among his clients are *Domus* magazine, the Institute of Directors, Museum on Thames. He is design consultant to Phaidon Press. In 1993 he was awarded The Prince Philip Prize for Designer of the Year.

VINCE FROST

Vince Frost began his career as a freelance designer working for Howard Brown and then for Pentagram Design. In 1989 he joined Pentagram on a full-time basis to work with John Rushworth on projects for Polaroid. In 1992, at 27, he became Pentagram's youngest associate and with a dedicated team of designers ran programmes for The Craft's Council, Sadler's Wells and The Royal Shakespeare Company. In November 1994 he formed Frost Design. He is presently working on a program of portfolios and a bulletin for Magnum Photos, and he designs and art directs D&AD's newsletter.

MARK GEER

Mark Geer is a principal of Geer Design, Inc., a communications firm based in Houston. Established in 1983, his firm specializes in annual reports, publication design and identity programs serving a broad range of clients which include Fortune 500 corporations, major universities, and non-profit institutions in the US and Canada. Mark's work has been recognized by the AIGA, New York Art Directors Club, and Mead Annual Report Show. His work is also included in the Merrill Berman Collection of Twentieth Century Modernist Art and Graphic Design.

ANGUS HYLAND

Angus Hyland studied at the London College of Printing and graduated in 1988 from the Royal College of Art. Since then he has worked freelance in England and Europe and in collaboration with the designers Louise Cantrill and Silvia Gaspardo-Moro. His work has been published and exhibited both nationally and internationally. He currently runs his own studio from Soho, London.

JEFF JOHNSON

Jeff Johnson is from North Dakota. In 1992, Jeff began working at Joe Duffy Design. He's since worked for such clients as Lee Jeans, The Coca-Cola Company, Stroh Brewery, Trailmark, and The Keith Haring Estate. When asked to define his position, his response is "navigator of the culture of materials." He's had work showcased in various media including *I.D.*, *Graphis*, *Communication Arts*, and *Smithsonian*. Jeff prefers to talk about design in terms of a verb rather than a noun.

KAN TAI-KEUNG

Born in 1942 in China, Tai-keung Kan moved to Hong Kong in 1957. In 1967 he started his career in design. In 1976 he co-founded SS Design & Production with partners; in 1988 he headed the company in partnership with Freeman Lau, and the company is now known as Kan & Lau Design Consultants. Kan has received over four hundred awards in international competitions.

ALAN KITCHING

Alan Kitching, RDI, is a designer and art director. He is the creator of letterpress typographic images for advertising, editorial design, and exhibition. He is a designer and printer of limited edition prints and specialty books at his typography workshop in London. In 1988 he was appointed head of letterpress typography at the Royal College of Art. In 1989 he established "The Typography Workshop" in Clerkenwell, London. In 1994 he was appointed Royal Designer for Industry (RDI), and elected member of *Alliance Graphique Internationale* (AGI).

KOEWEIDEN POSTMA ASSOC.

Koeweiden Postma Associates was founded in 1987, and is based in Amsterdam. Its principals are Jacques Koeweiden (right), creative director, Paul Postma (left), creative director, and Dick De Groot, managing director. Clients include Nike Europe, Heineken, Chiat-Day London, DDB Needham Amsterdam, and Glaxo. The company has received awards from the British D&AD; Art Directors Club of New York; TDC Tokyo; One Show USA; and the Dutch Art Directors Club.

UWE LOESCH

Uwe Loesch was born in 1943 in Germany where he studied and maintains a design studio. He is a member of the Alliance Graphique Internationale, the Type Directors Club of New York and the Art Directors Club of Germany. He has taught at the University of Wuppertal. He has has exhibited in Germany, France, Japan, Hong Kong, Indonesia and Brazil and has won numerous awards for his poster designs. Since 1984 his work is in the collection of the Museum of Modern Art in New York.

ITALO LUPI

A graduate in architecture from the Polytechnic of Milan, and a member of AGI (*Alliance Graphic Internationale*), Italo Lupi has worked, since 1972, in the field of Graphic design. Art director of *Domus* magazine for six years, he is now editor and art director of *Abitare* magazine. Lupi designs for private firms, publishing houses, social and political enterprises; he designs exhibitions, museums, and scenery.

THOMAS MANSS

Thomas Manss began his career at Erik Spiekermann's Metadesign in Berlin where he was involved in the development of the Berlin Transport information system and designed exhibition catalogues for the Kunstamt Kreuzberg. In 1985 he moved to Sedley Place Design where he ran design programmes for such companies as Volkswagen, Votex, Schering, Deutsche Bundespost and Deutsche Bundesbank. He joined Pentagram in 1989 and collaborated with Alan Fletcher. In 1992 he was made an associate, and in 1993 he left Pentagram to open his own studio in London. His clients include BMW, the Institute of Directors, Phaidon Press, and Ritz Carlton of Spain.

Note: The photos and bios of the following contributers can be found on their self-designed spreads: Derek Birdsall, A.G. Fronzoni, David Kampa (photo only), Theo Leuthold, and D.J. Stout.

PIERRE MENDELL

Pierre Mendell lived in France until 1947, when he emigrated to the US and became an American citizen. From 1958 to 1960 he studied graphic design with Armin Hofmann in Basel. With Klaus Oberer he founded the studio Mendell & Oberer in Munich in 1961. The work of the studio encompasses the development of corporate identities, poster design, book and packaging design, signage systems, and architectural graphics.

TOON MICHIELS

Toon Michiels has been a designer and photographer since 1973. In the 1970s he worked as a graphic designer for, among others, Anthon Beeke and Eelco Bos. In the early 1980s he started his own studio in Amsterdam and Hertogenbosch. He designs posters and programs for the Dutch Opera and VARA Matinee. He received four ADCN awards for his designs and illustrations in the literary supplement of *Avenue* magazine. He lives and works in Hertogenbosch, The Netherlands.

BRUNO MONGUZZI

Bruno Monguzzi was born in Ticino, the Italian part of Switzerland, in 1941. He has studied graphic design in Geneva, typography, photography, and Gestalt psychology in London. In the early 1960s he joined Studio Boggeri in Milan and has lectured in typographic design at the Cini Foundation in Venice. After designing nine pavillions for Expo 67 in Montreal, he returned to Milan in 1968 to work mainly in book, poster, and exhibit design. He was elected best Swiss Typographer of the Year in 1994.

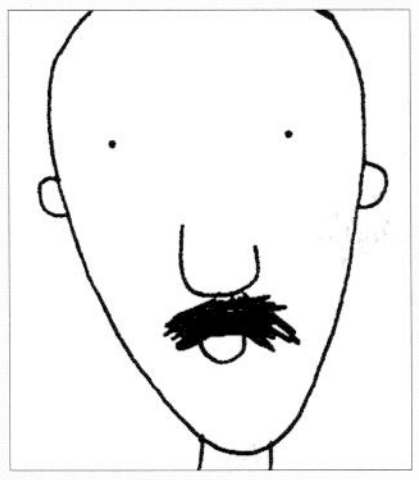

QUENTIN NEWARK

Quentin Newark started his career at Faber and Faber Publishers designing the insides of novels. After concerted pleading he joined Pentagram, continuing to design all the Faber and Faber book covers with John McConnell. Alan Fletcher nodded to him one evening and it began a five-year working relationship, including the livery for the Victoria & Albert Museum. He left to set up Atelier Works with John Powner, also ex-Pentagram. Projects include art direction of *Design*, journal of the Design Council, catalogues for the National Portrait Gallery, a photography exhibition for Citibank, and a how-to manual with Sir Norman Foster and Partners.

ROBERT PETRICK

Robert Petrick graduated from the University of Cincinnati's College of Design, Architecture and Art in 1978. From the mid-1970s through the mid-1980s he worked in various environments as art director, designer, copywriter, and design manager. In 1986, he formed the office of Petrick Design in Chicago. Petrick Design is recognized globally for its work and locally for its Great Dane.

WOODY PIRTLE

Woody Pirtle came to Pentagram in 1988 as a partner following ten years of running his own successful practice in Dallas and earlier training at The Richards Group. He has produced identity and publication designs for clients like PrimeCo., United Technologies, Nine West, Northern Telecom, Rizzoli Publishing, *Upper and Lower Case*, Simpson Paper Company and the Rockefeller Foundation. His work has been exhibited wordwide and is in the permanent collections of the Museum of Modern Art and Cooper-Hewitt Museum in New York, the Victoria & Albert Museum in London, the Neue Sammlung Museum in Munich, and the Zurich Poster Museum.

NEIL POWELL

As Design Director of Duffy Design's newly opened New York office, Neil's work includes brand and corporate identity development for clients such as BMW, The Lee Apparel Company, Jim Beam Brands, The Stroh Brewery Company, The Coca-Cola Company, Minute Maid, Beckett Papers, and Faith Popcorn's BrainReserve.

LEX REITSMA

Lex Reitsma has worked as a freelance graphic designer since 1983. Starting in 1990 he designed all the programs and posters for the Dutch National Opera. In 1982 he received the Frans Duwaer Commission, in 1988 the basic award for the Prix de Rome for Graphic Design and in 1994 he received the Dutch Theater Poster Award. In the spring of 1997, the Dutch National Mail issued a stamp of his making.

LANA RIGSBY

Lana Rigsby is principical of Rigsby Design, Inc. Based in Houston, Texas, the company specializes in corporate communications and identity development. The firm's work is included in the permanent collection of the Smithsonian Institution, and is consistently recognized by major design competitions and publications. Lana is a past officer and founding member of the Texas chapter of the American Institute of Graphic Arts and was named *Adweek's* Southwest Creative All-Star Designer for 1994. She chaired the 1996 Mead Annual Report Conference, and serves as director of the Eran Wilder Samata Foundation.

PAULA SCHER

Paula Scher consulted independently for one year before joining Pentagram as a partner in April 1991. She has developed identity systems, promotional materials, packaging and publication designs that have repositioned products, services, and institutions. Her clients have included RCA Consumer Electronics, Children's Television Workshop, *The New York Times Magazine*, Champion International Corporation, Estee Lauder, The Public Theater, and The American Museum of Natural History. Her work is represented in the collections of New York's Museum of Modern Art, the Zurich Poster Museum, the Denver Art Museum, and the Centre Georges Pompidou, Paris.

NANCY SKOLOS

Nancy Skolos has worked with her husband, the photographer Thomas Wedell, as a partner since 1980 in Skolos/Wedell, a Boston-based interdisciplinary design and photo studio. They have produced posters and corporate literature for high technology and electronics companies including Digital Equipment Corporation, Boston Acoustics, Closs Video Corporation, as wells as clients such as EMI Music Publishing, The Walker Art Center, and the Lyceum Fellowship in Architecture.

ERIK SPIEKERMANN

Erik Spiekermann financed his studies in Art History at Berlin's Free University by running a printing press and setting metal type in the basement of his house. After spending seven years as a freelance designer in London, he returned to Berlin in 1979, where — together with two partners — he founded MetaDesign. Now the largest design studio in Germany, MetaDesign now has offices in San Francisco and London. Worldwide clients include Adobe, Apple, Audi, Boehringer, Hewlett Packard, IBM, and Texas Instruments.

CHITTAMAI SUVONGESE

Chittamai "Kobe" Suvongese received his BFA in Visual Communication Design from Silpakorn University in Dankok, Thailand. He then graduated with a Masters degree in graphic design from Iowa State University in 1985. He moved to Minneapolis in 1985 and worked at Design Center. In 1992, Kobe joined Joe Duffy Design as a senior designer responsible for many clients including The Coca-Cola Company, Chums LTD., Jim Beam Brands, The Phillips Beverage Company, and Stroh Brewery.

STEVE SANDSTROM

Steve Sandstrom is Creative Director and a principal of Sandstrom Design, a nine-person firm, in Portland, Oregon. Recent clients have included Levi Strauss & Co., Nike Design, Pavlov Productions, ESPN, Nissan Pathfinder, Microsoft, BMG, Cloetta (Sweden), Miller Brewing Co., Wieden & Kennedy, TBWA/Chiat Day, and Foote Cone and Belding/SF. In 1994 he was named Advertising Professional of the Year by the Portland Advertising Federation. He also won a blue ribbon (while in first grade) at the Oregon State Fair for a crayon drawing of a cow.

MICHAEL VANDERBYL

Michael Vanderbyl received a BFA degree in Graphic Design from the College of Arts and Crafts in 1968. Today he is Dean of the School of Design at his alma mater. Since establishing Vanderbyl Design in 1973, he has gained international prominence in the design field as a practitioner, educator, critic and advocate. He has been a visiting instructor at Cranbrook Academy of Art, University of Cincinnati, Kent State University, Art Institute of Chicago and the Universities of Kansas and Washington. He is a frequent juror for prominent international design competitions.

JOVICA VELJOVIC

Jovica Veljovic lives in Germany, teaches type design and calligraphy at the Fachhochschule Hamburg, and teaches workshops throughout Europe and the United States. He has designed three typefaces for the International Typeface Corporation: ITC Veljovic, ITC Esprit, and ITC Gamma, and has served as a consultant on Cyrillic type designs for Apple Computer, Inc., Linotype-Hell AG, and URW Software & Type. In 1985 he received the Charles Peignot Award from the Association Typographique Internationale for excellence in calligraphy and type design.

JEAN WIDMER

Jean Widmer moved to Paris from Switzerland in 1953 to study at the Ecole des Beaux-Arts. He established his own studio, Visual Design, in 1970. His credits include the redesign of the tourist and cultural route signs in France (still in progress) and corporate identity programs for cultural institutions such as the Bibliothèque Nationale. In 1994 Widmer received the *Grand Prix National des Arts Graphiques* and in 1996 a retrospective of his work was shown at the *Centre Georges Pompidou*.

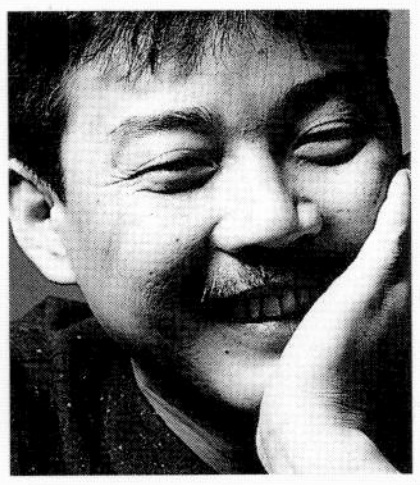

WANG XU

Wang Xu was born in 1955. In 1979 he graduated from the Design Department of Guangzhou Fine Arts College, Guangzhou, China. In 1986 he went to Hong Kong to take up graphic design as a profession and in 1995 he returned to Guangzhou and founded Wang Xu & Associates Ltd. Since 1986 Wang Xu has edited and designed eleven issues of *Design Exchange* magazine, a Chinese/English bilingual publication that introduces trends in graphic design.

Photo Credits: Baines: Drawing by Nigel Robinson Bos: Photo by Koos Breukel Fotografie Cerri: Photo by Orietta Ferrero Fletcher: Photo by Martin Dunkerton Geer: Photo by Terry Vine Photography Kitching: Drawing by Ron Sanford Lupi: Photo by Luigi Ronchi Rigsby: Photo by Chris Shinn Scher: Photo by Peter Harrison Michiels: Photo by W.J. Kersten Pirtle: Photo by Richard Frank

Graphis319

Jennifer Morla
Frank Gehry
Soo Kim
Weiss Stagliano
Ron Arad
Tibor Kalman
Mary Ellen Mark

Graphis319

Morla

MORLA / GEHRY / KIM /WEISS STAGLIANO /ARAD / KALMAN / MARK

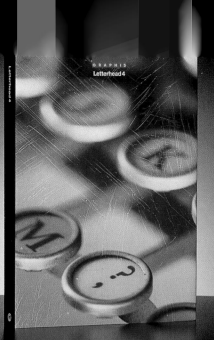

GRAPHIS
Letterhead 4

Design Annual 1999

GRAPHIS
Digital Photo 1

Brochures 3

GRAPHIS
Corporate Identity 3

GRAPHIS
Annual Reports 6

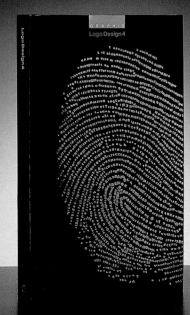

Logo Design 4

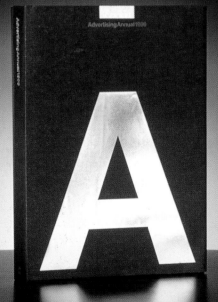

Advertising Annual 1998

GRAPHIS
T-shirt Design 2

Order Form

We're introducing a great way to reward Graphis magazine readers: If you subscribe to Graphis, you'll qualify for a 40% discount on our books. If you subscribe and place a Standing Order, you'll get a 50% discount on our books. A Standing Order means we'll reserve your selected Graphis Annual or Series title(s) at press, and ship it to you at 50% discount. With a Standing Order for Design Annual 1999, for example, you'll receive this title at half off, and each coming year, we'll send you the newest Design Annual at this low price—an ideal way for the professional to keep informed, year after year. In addition to the titles here, we carry books in all communication disciplines, so call if there's another title we can get for you. Thank you for supporting Graphis.

Book title	Order No.	Retail	40% off Discount	standing order 50% off	Quantity	Totals
Advertising Annual 1999	1500	☐ $70.00	☐ $42.00	☐ $35.00		
Annual Reports 6 (s)	1550	☐ $70.00	☐ $42.00	☐ $35.00		
Apple Design	1259	☐ $45.00	☐ $27.00	N/A		
Black & White Blues	4710	☐ $40.00	☐ $24.00	N/A		
Book Design 2 (s)	1453	☐ $70.00	☐ $42.00	☐ $35.00		
Brochures 3 (s)	1496	☐ $70.00	☐ $42.00	☐ $35.00		
Corporate Identity 3 (s)	1437	☐ $70.00	☐ $42.00	☐ $35.00		
Design Annual 1999	1488	☐ $70.00	☐ $42.00	☐ $35.00		
Digital Photo 1 (s)	1593	☐ $70.00	☐ $42.00	☐ $35.00		
Ferenc Berko	1445	☐ $60.00	☐ $36.00	N/A		
Information Architects	1380	☐ $35.00	☐ $21.00	N/A		
Interactive Design 1 (s)	1631	☐ $70.00	☐ $42.00	☐ $35.00		
Letterhead 4 (s)	1577	☐ $70.00	☐ $42.00	☐ $35.00		
Logo Design 4 (s)	1585	☐ $60.00	☐ $36.00	☐ $30.00		
New Talent Design Annual 1999	1607	☐ $60.00	☐ $36.00	☐ $30.00		
Nudes 1	212	☐ $50.00	☐ $30.00	N/A		
Passion & Line	1372	☐ $50.00	☐ $30.00	N/A		
Photo Annual 1998	1461	☐ $70.00	☐ $42.00	☐ $35.00		
Pool Light	1470	☐ $70.00	☐ $42.00	N/A		
Poster Design Annual 1998	1410	☐ $70.00	☐ $42.00	N/A		
Poster Design Annual 1999	1623	☐ $70.00	☐ $42.00	☐ $35.00		
Product Design 2 (s)	1330	☐ $70.00	☐ $42.00	☐ $35.00		
Promotion Design 1 (s)	1615	☐ $70.00	☐ $42.00	☐ $35.00		
T-Shirt Design 2 (s)	1402	☐ $60.00	☐ $36.00	☐ $30.00		
Walter Iooss	1569	☐ $60.00	☐ $36.00	N/A		
World Trademarks	1070	☐ $250.00	☐ $150.00	N/A		

Shipping & handling per book, US $7.00, Canada $15.00, International $20.00.

New York State shipments add 8.25% tax.

Standing Orders I understand I am committing to the selected annuals and/or series and will be automatically charged for each new volume in forthcoming years, at 50% off. I must call and cancel my order when I am no longer interested in purchasing the book. (To honor your standing order discount you must sign below.)

_____   _____
Signature   Date

Graphis magazine	☐ One year subscription	USA $90	Canada $125	Int'l $125	
	☐ Two year subscription	USA $165	Canada $235	Int'l $235	
	☐ One year student*	USA $75	Canada $90	Int'l $90	
	☐ Single or Back Issues (per)	USA $24	Canada $28	Int'l $28	

*All students must mail a copy of student ID along with the order form.   **(s)** = series (published every 2-4 years)

Name	☐ American Express ☐ Visa ☐ Mastercard ☐ Check
Company	
Address	Card #
City State Zip	Expiration
Daytime phone	Card holder's signature

Send this order form (or copy) and make check payable to Graphis Inc. For even faster turn-around service, or if you have any questions about subscribing, call us at the following numbers: in the US (800) 209. 4234; outside the US (212) 532. 9387 ext. 242 or 241; fax (212) 696. 4242. Mailing address: Graphis, 141 Lexington Avenue, New York, New York 10016-8193. Order Graphis on the Web from anywhere in the world: <www.graphis.com>.

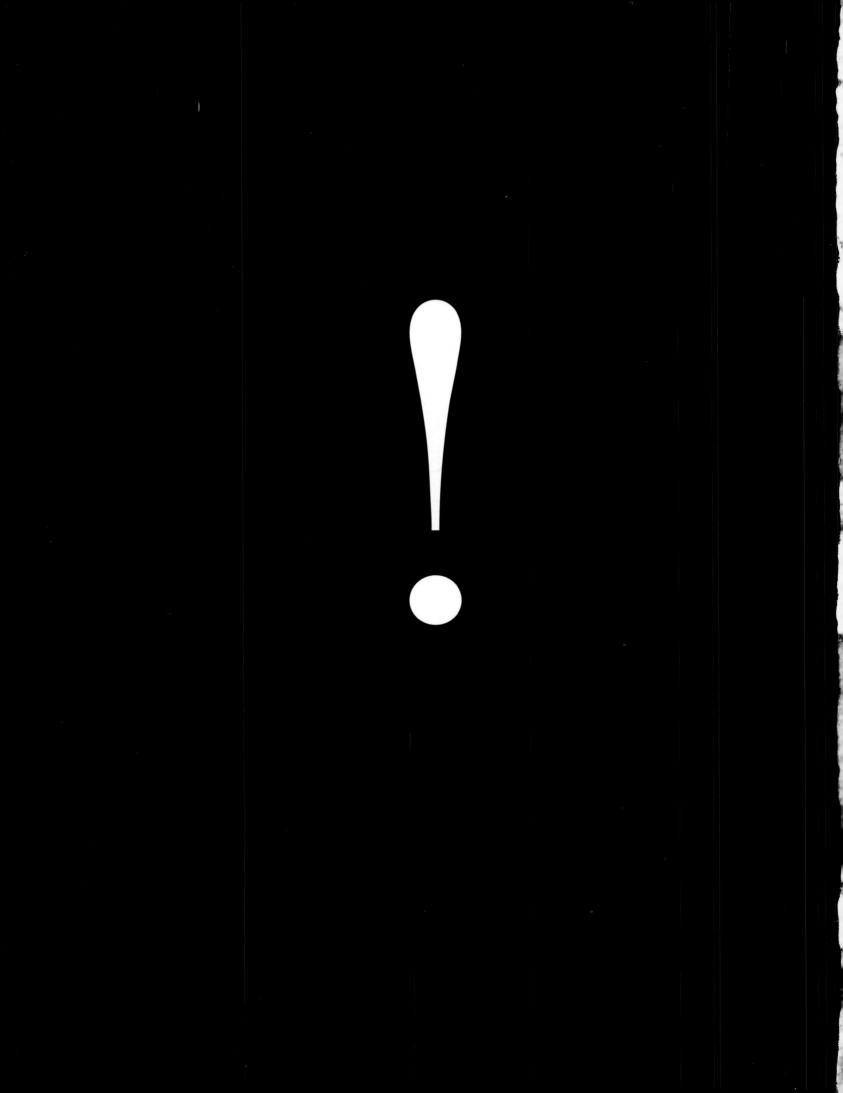